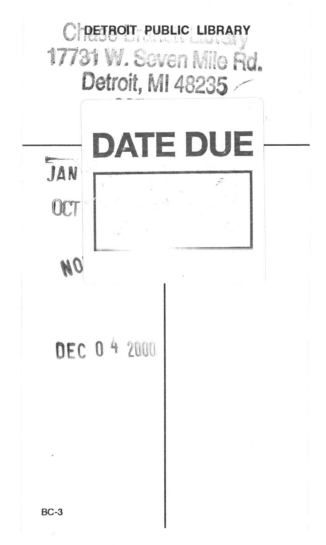

THE STORY ATLAS
OF THE BIBLE

ELROSE HUNTER

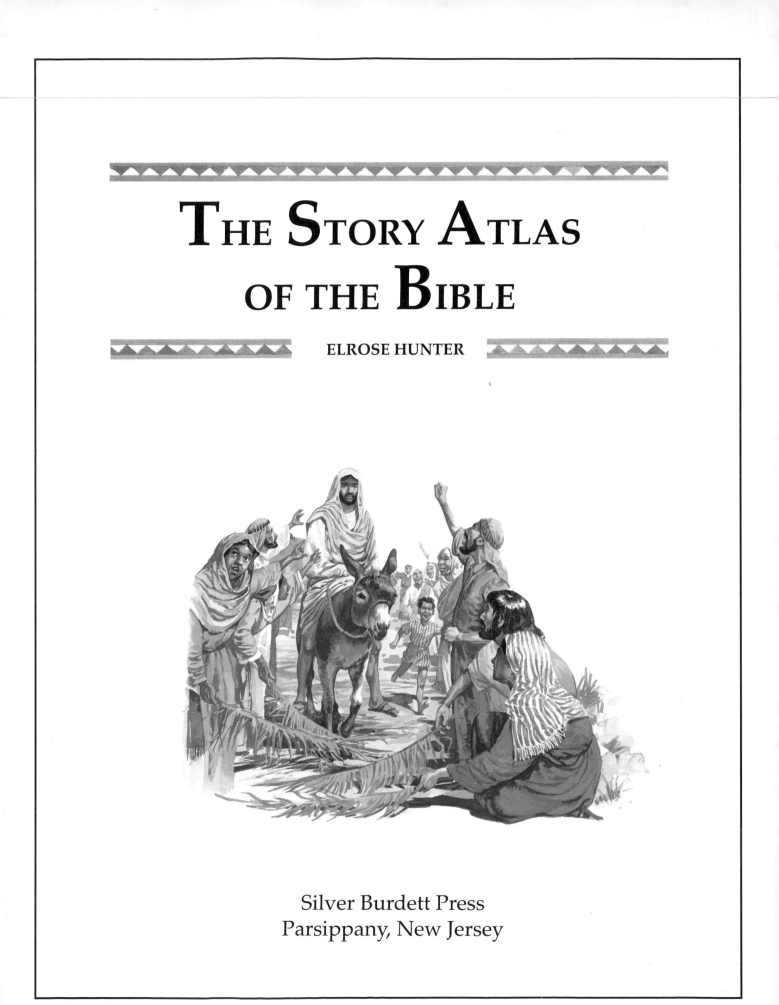

Silver Burdett Press
Parsippany, New Jersey

Illustrated by

Mike Foster (*Maltings Partnership*)
Julian Baker
Adam Hook, Roger Payne, Clive Spong (*Linden Artists*)
Richard Berridge, Julia Pearson (*Specs Art*)
Mark Viney (*Allied Artists*)
Tony Smith (*Virgil Pomfret Agency*)

Consultant editor: Judith Merrell

First published in 1994 by Scripture Union
130 City Road London EC1V 2NJ

Planned and produced by: Andromeda Oxford Limited
11-15 The Vineyard Abingdon Oxon OX14 3PX

Text © 1996 this edition by Silver Burdett Press

Published in the United States in 1996 by Silver Burdett Press,
A Simon and Schuster Company
299 Jefferson Road
Parsippany, NJ 07054

Printed in Slovenia
10 9 8 7 6 5 4 3 2 1

Library of Congress Cataloging-in-Publication Data
Hunter, Elrose.
The story atlas of the Bible / Elrose Hunter; illustrated by Mike Foster . . . [et al.].
p. cm.
ISBN 0-382-39102-0 (LSB) ISBN 0-382-39103-9 (pbk.)
1. Bible--History of Biblical events--Juvenile literature.
2. Bible--Geography--Maps.
3. Bible--Geography--Juvenile literature.
[1. Bible--History of Biblical events.
2. Bible--Geography] I. Foster, Mike (Mike Stuart), ill. II. Title
BS621.H86 1995 94-404789
220.91--dc20 CIP AC

CONTENTS

THE WORLD OF THE BIBLE

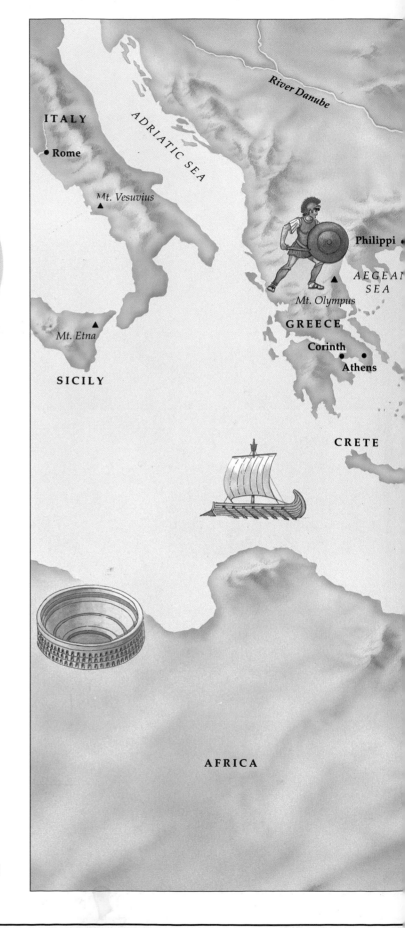

If we follow the Bible story from when the world began to Paul's travels to spread the Christian faith, we are taken on a long journey over thousands of miles—westward from the Middle East to the lands that surround the Mediterranean Sea. It may not look a large area when we see it on our world map today, but to people of the time, well over two thousand years ago, travel over these lands was much slower. So the distances seemed vast.

We are also going on a journey back in time, because the events in the Bible stretch back over four thousand years.

MEDITERRANEAN WORLD

The events in the Bible took place around the Mediterranean and in the Middle East (above). This part of the world was the center of civilization in Bible times. During the history of the Old and New Testaments, five nations in turn became powerful empires: the Assyrians, the Babylonians, the Persians, the Greeks and the Romans (right).

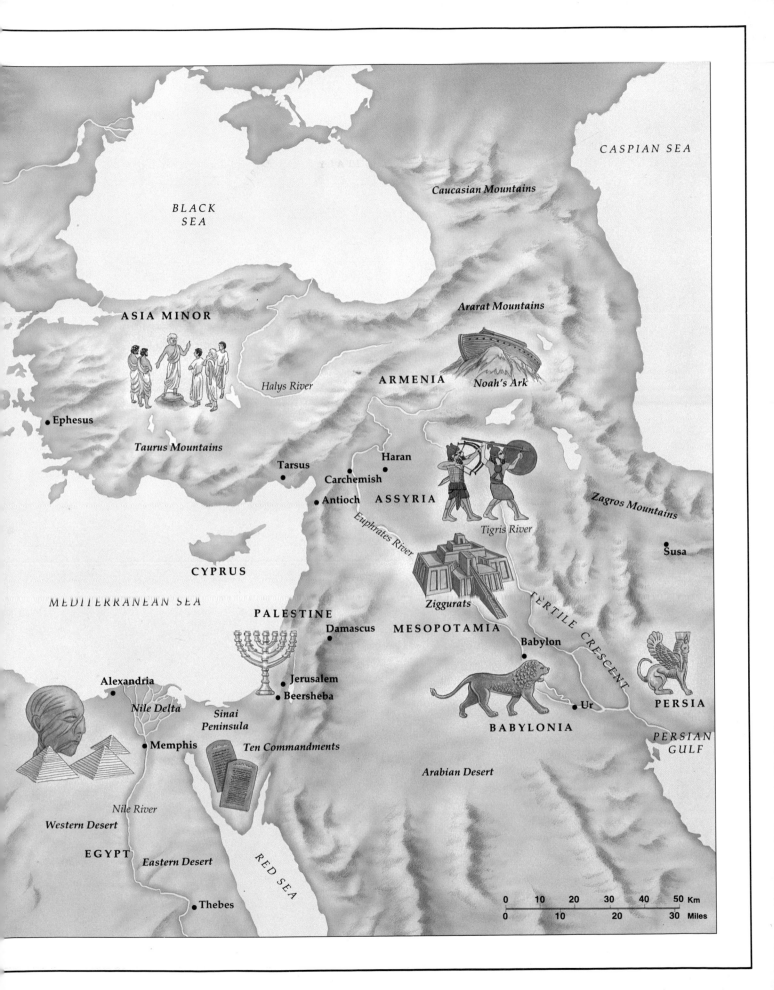

BLACK
SEA

CASPIAN SEA

Caucasian Mountains

Ararat Mountains

ASIA MINOR

ARMENIA

Noah's Ark

Halys River

Ephesus

Taurus Mountains

Haran

Tarsus

Carchemish

Zagros Mountains

Antioch

ASSYRIA

CYPRUS

Susa

Tigris River

Euphrates River

MEDITERRANEAN SEA

Ziggurats

PALESTINE

MESOPOTAMIA

Damascus

FERTILE CRESCENT

Babylon

PERSIA

Alexandria

Jerusalem

Nile Delta

Beersheba

Ur

Sinai
Peninsula

Memphis

Ten Commandments

BABYLONIA

PERSIAN
GULF

Arabian Desert

Nile River

Western Desert

EGYPT

Eastern Desert

RED SEA

Thebes

| 0 | 10 | 20 | 30 | 40 | 50 Km |
| 0 | | 10 | 20 | | 30 Miles |

OUR BIBLE JOURNEY

Our journey begins in Mesopotamia, a land sometimes called the "Cradle of Civilization." The fertile lands fed by two rivers, the Tigris and Euphrates, made it possible for people to settle there, grow crops, and build cities.

We set out with Abraham from the city of Ur about 2000 B.C. and travel the "Fertile Crescent" to the land of Canaan. Abraham, and his descendants Isaac and Jacob, were nomads in Canaan. This meant they lived in tents and moved from place to place in search of water and pasture for their flocks of sheep and goats. God promised Abraham that the land of Canaan would belong to his descendants, and the country became known as the "Promised Land."

From Canaan we travel south to Egypt. We arrive there with Joseph, who starts off as a slave and ends up becoming the Pharaoh's governor. The pyramids had been built about a thousand years earlier, and Egypt had a long history of civilization.

We stay in Egypt for several hundred years. During this time the descendants of Joseph become the nation of Israelites. They are made slaves by the Egyptians. Shortly after the time of Tutankhamen, Moses is born. He is to rescue the Israelites and lead them away from Egypt across the desert back to the Promised Land.

When they eventually enter the land and capture the first city, Jericho, it is the start of a long period of conquest. The Canaanites and the Philistines, already in the land, have to be conquered and driven out.

By 1000 B.C. King David and King Solomon have extended the Israelites' territory, and for a time there is peace. But then a shadow creeps slowly across from the east as the mighty empires of first Assyria and then Babylonia grow stronger and seize more lands.

We journey on from the ruins of Jerusalem in 586 B.C. with thousands of prisoners of war, like Daniel, into exile in Babylonia. After seventy years when the exiles are allowed to return home, we go back to Jerusalem and see Nehemiah organize the rebuilding of the city.

We end our Old Testament journey with the land of Israel becoming part of the Greek Empire, when Alexander the Great conquers the civilized world.

After a gap of about three hundred years, we take up our travels into the New Testament when the Romans have made Palestine part of their empire. Augustus is emperor when Jesus is born in Bethlehem.

We follow in the footsteps of Jesus, staying within the land of Palestine. We journey with him around the towns and villages of Galilee where we see him teaching and healing.

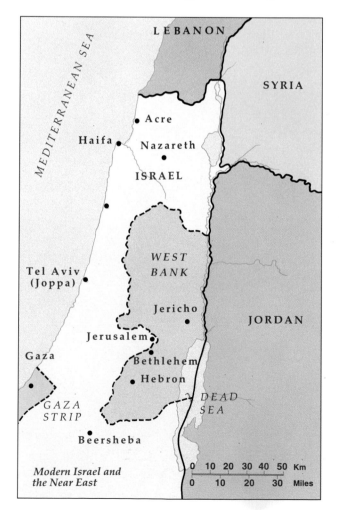

Modern Israel and
the Near East

We head south with Jesus to Jerusalem where he is arrested, tried, and put to death. We finally follow his disciples taking the gospel beyond the borders of Palestine (notably Paul as far as Europe), after Jesus has risen.

PROMISED LAND: OLD AND NEW

The land known by various names in its history as Canaan, the Promised Land, Israel, and Palestine, is the setting for most of our stories. It occupies a key position linking Africa and Asia like a bridge. But it is a small country—only about 175 miles from north to south, and about half that distance from west to east. There are four main geographical regions: the Coastal Plain, Central Highlands, Jordan Rift Valley, and Eastern Plateau. The map of the same area (below, left) shows locations today.

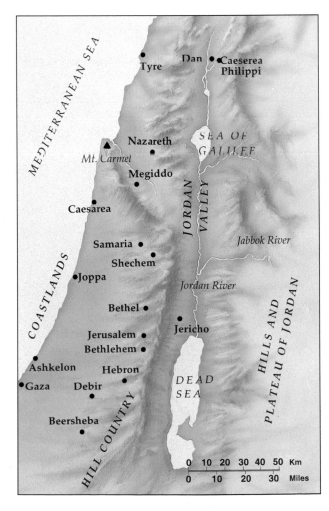

TRAVEL IN THE BIBLE WORLD

In Bible times most land journeys were on foot or on the backs of animals such as donkeys and camels. Wooden-wheeled wagons pulled by donkeys or oxen were used as early as the time of Abraham. Horses appeared later but were owned only by kings and warriors. King Solomon had stables for several thousand horses. The horse was used mainly for pulling war chariots.

Roads were developed as empires grew. The Persian kings built the Royal Road from their capital city of Susa west for 1600 miles to the city of Sardis in Asia Minor. They organized a system of posting stations, placing horses and messengers a day's journey apart all along the road. Official letters could be handed down the line and took only three weeks to deliver between Susa and Sardis.

But it was the Romans who set up the greatest network of roads in Bible lands, right across their empire.

By the first century after Jesus' death, many people moved freely across the Roman empire. This helped Paul and others to found Christian churches in Asia Minor and Europe and to keep in touch by letter.

Most of the lands of the Bible border the Mediterranean Sea. There was travel, too, by water from the earliest times. The Egyptians sailed up and down the Nile River and also built sea-going ships for travel across the Mediterranean. Over a thousand years before Jesus, the Phoenicians, who lived on the coast north of Palestine, were adventurous sailors and explored westward to Europe and south around Africa.

The Israelites were not really seafaring people, partly because their coastline has no safe, natural harbors. It was not until Roman times, when a harbor was built at Caesarea, that regular trade by sea was established.

LONG AGO WHEN THE WORLD BEGAN

GENESIS 1–11

IN THE beginning, when God created Adam and Eve, he planted a beautiful garden for them to enjoy. A stream watered the Garden of Eden, and all kinds of flowers and trees grew there.

Adam and Eve tended the garden and ate the fruit from the trees. But God told them not to eat the fruit of one particular tree. One day they disobeyed God and ate the fruit. So he sent them away from the Garden of Eden. From then on Adam and Eve had to work hard to grow food for themselves as well as their family.

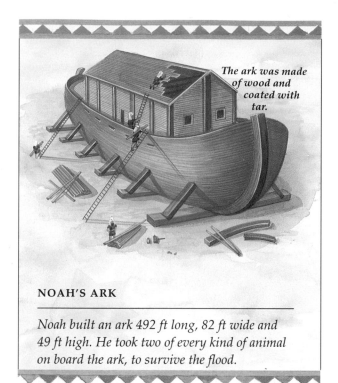

The ark was made of wood and coated with tar.

NOAH'S ARK

Noah built an ark 492 ft long, 82 ft wide and 49 ft high. He took two of every kind of animal on board the ark, to survive the flood.

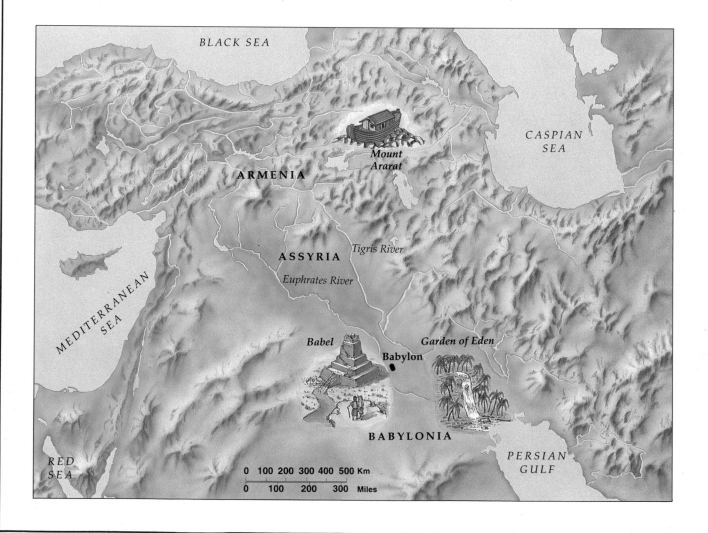

Many years passed and the number of people on the Earth grew. They ignored God and became evil and violent. God was sorry that he had put them on the Earth, and he decided to start again. But he made an agreement with a good man, Noah, that he would keep him and his family alive, and also two of every kind of animal.

Noah followed God's instructions and built a great boat. When it was ready and all were on board, rain fell for forty days and forty nights. Only those on the boat survived the flood that covered the land.

As the flood waters went down, the boat came to rest on Mount Ararat. When Noah and his family and all the animals left the boat, God made a rainbow appear in the sky. It was a sign of his promise that he would never again destroy the world by a flood.

Noah's sons—Shem, Ham and Japeth—became the ancestors of all the nations of the world. Years passed and the descendants of Noah settled on a plain in Babylonia. They had discovered how to make bricks with mud and tar, and they decided to build a city with a tower to reach the sky. "If we do this, we will become famous." they said.

God looked at their tower. "These people think they do not need me," God said, and he mixed up their language so they could not understand each other and could not build the city together. God scattered the people with their new languages across the Earth. The Tower of Babel was never finished.

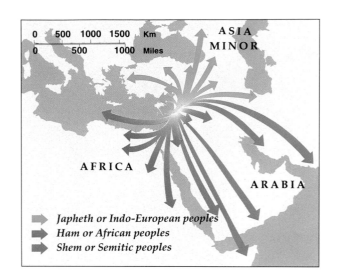

Japheth or Indo-European peoples
Ham or African peoples
Shem or Semitic peoples

GROWTH OF THE NATIONS

Noah's sons and their descendants spread out to fill the world with many different peoples (above).

THE TOWER OF BABEL

God punished the people for building the tower by jumbling their language, so they could not talk to one another (below).

IN THE BEGINNING

God created the Garden of Eden and filled it with all kinds of plants and creatures. The land was extremely fertile and was watered by rivers, including the Tigris and Euphrates (left).

ABRAHAM AND THE PROMISED LAND

GENESIS 11–24

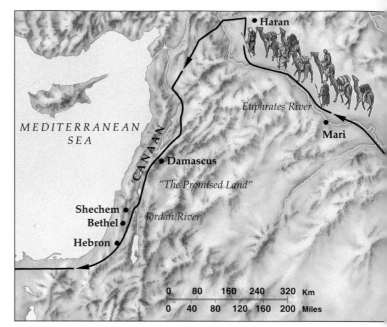

ABRAHAM WAS born in the city of Ur in Mesopotamia about 2,000 years before the time of Jesus. The people of Ur lived in mud-brick houses, traded with far-off lands, and worshiped the Moon god.

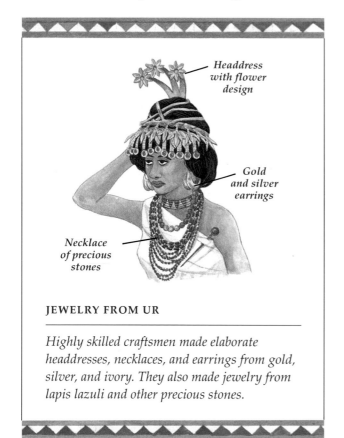

JEWELRY FROM UR

Highly skilled craftsmen made elaborate headdresses, necklaces, and earrings from gold, silver, and ivory. They also made jewelry from lapis lazuli and other precious stones.

Labels on jewelry illustration:
- Headdress with flower design
- Gold and silver earrings
- Necklace of precious stones

THE JOURNEYS OF ABRAHAM

Abraham probably followed the main trade routes from Ur and Haran to Canaan, the land God had promised him and his descendants. These routes usually stayed close to rivers and settlements (above).

Abraham's father decided to leave Ur, and the family headed northwest along the Euphrates River. They settled in Haran and there God spoke to Abraham. "Leave your home and go to a land that I will show you. There your descendants will become a great nation."

Abraham and his wife, Sarah, lived in tents as they traveled south to the land of Canaan. Abraham was wealthy, and they had servants and flocks of livestock. They lived a nomadic life, camping wherever they found water and pasture and moving on again.

Abraham's nephew, Lot, traveled with them. He also had his family and servants as well as sheep, goats, and cattle. The time came when there was not enough pasture land for the two of them to stay together. Quarrels broke out between the herdspeople.

Abraham decided it was time to separate. He said to Lot, "Choose which part of the land

THE NOMADIC LIFE

Abraham's tent would have been made of goat's hair cloth. A curtain divided the tent into two rooms: one for the men, the other for the women and children (below).

Abraham's journeys

Babylon

Tigris River

Ur
Temple to Moon god

you want, and I'll go the opposite way."

Lot chose the green pastures of the Jordan valley, where there was plenty of water, and headed east. Abraham settled in the hilly country near Hebron. There God spoke to him again. "Look around you to the north, south, east, and west. This is the land I promised to give you and your descendants."

Sarah and Abraham wondered about God's promise as they grew older and had no children. But when they were quite old, God gave them a son. Abraham and Sarah loved their only son, Isaac, dearly.

When Isaac grew up, Abraham sent his most trusted servant back to Haran to choose a wife for Isaac from among his relatives. The servant brought back Rebecca, the daughter of Abraham's nephew. Isaac fell in love with her, and Rebecca was welcomed into Abraham's family.

JACOB AND ESAU: THE SHEPHERD AND THE HUNTER

GENESIS 25–35

SOME YEARS after Isaac married Rebecca, they had twin sons, Jacob and Esau. Esau loved the outdoor life and became a hunter. He was Isaac's favorite while Rebecca preferred the quieter Jacob.

When the country of Canaan suffered famine, Isaac and his family moved to Gerar in Philistia, where the land was fertile. He prospered and grew so rich that the Philistines became jealous of him. So Isaac decided that it was time to move back to the land God had promised to his father Abraham and his descendants. Isaac made a peace treaty with the king of the Philistines, and he settled in Beersheba.

Years passed and Isaac grew old and blind. One day he sent Esau out hunting. "Cook my favorite meat. When I have eaten it, I will give you my blessing before I die."

Rebecca overheard him and plotted with Jacob to cheat Esau. Jacob pretended to be Esau and deceived his father into giving him the blessing meant for Esau. From then on, Esau planned to kill Jacob. When Rebecca found out, she urged Jacob to go and stay with his uncle, Laban, in Haran for a while.

On his long trek north to Haran, Jacob slept under the stars at night. One night he dreamed he saw a stairway of angels reaching to heaven, and he heard God saying to him, "I will protect and be with you wherever you go and bring you back to this land." Next morning Jacob vowed he would come back to this spot one day and worship God. He named the place Bethel, meaning "House of God."

When Jacob reached Haran, he met Rachel, Laban's daughter, at a well with her father's sheep. Jacob helped her to draw water.

JACOB AT THE WELL

Jacob rolled away the stone covering the well so Rachel could water her sheep. Wells were meeting places for village women as well as herdspeople (below).

NAMING SPECIAL PLACES

Piles of stones were often used to mark special places, for example, the spot where an agreement was settled or, like Jacob, places where the presence of God was felt.

Jacob used a stone to mark the spot where he dreamed of the angels. He poured olive oil over it, dedicating it to God.

Sometimes the stones were used to remind people that God was watching over them. When Jacob left Haran, he and Laban set up some stones at a place called Mizpah, meaning "place from which to watch."

Jacob's uncle, Laban, put him in charge of his flocks of sheep and goats. Jacob lived there for twenty years and married Laban's daughters, first Leah, then Rachel.

Although Jacob worked hard, Laban was grudging in his wages. Jacob found ways to outsmart Laban and became rich.

Eventually he knew it was time to return to his homeland. Would Esau still be angry, Jacob wondered anxiously. But Esau came from Edom to greet him and show that he had forgiven him.

Jacob and his family went to live at Bethel, and God gave him the name Israel. His twelve sons were to become the heads of tribes of the nation of Israel.

JACOB'S JOURNEYS

Jacob traveled about 400 miles on foot from his home in Beersheba to his uncle's home in Haran. It was 20 years before he returned with a family, servants, and herds of livestock (right).

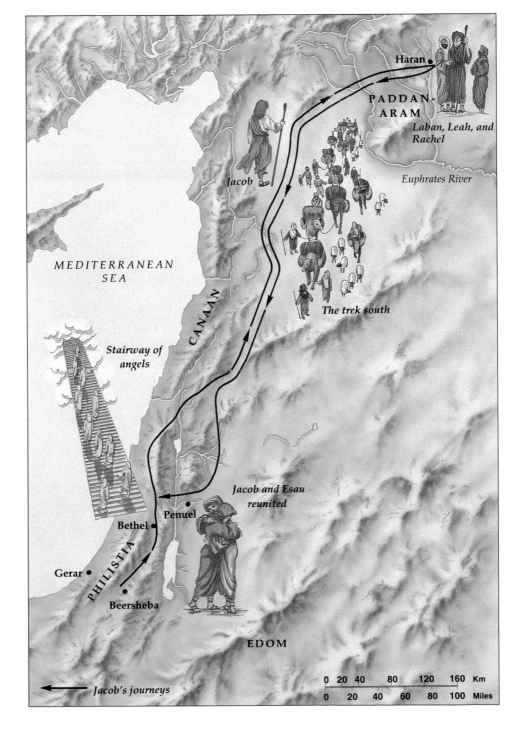

Haran

PADDAN-ARAM

Laban, Leah, and Rachel

Euphrates River

Jacob

MEDITERRANEAN SEA

CANAAN

The trek south

Stairway of angels

Jacob and Esau reunited

Penuel

Bethel

Gerar •

PHILISTIA

Beersheba

EDOM

| 0 | 20 | 40 | | 80 | | 120 | | 160 | Km |
| 0 | | 20 | 40 | | 60 | | 80 | | 100 | Miles |

← *Jacob's journeys*

JOSEPH THE DREAMER

GENESIS 37–50

JOSEPH WAS Jacob's favorite son. His eleven brothers were jealous when his father gave him a special coat, and they hated him because he dreamed that they would bow before him. "Do you think you are going to be king?" they jeered.

One day Jacob sent Joseph to check on his brothers, who were looking after the sheep some way off. "Look! Here comes the dreamer," the brothers said. "Let's get rid of him." They threw Joseph into a dry well.

When some traders came by, heading for Egypt, the brothers sold him for twenty silver pieces. They killed a goat, stained Joseph's coat with blood, and took it back home. Jacob mourned the son he thought was dead.

In Egypt the traders sold Joseph to Potiphar, captain of the Pharaoh's guards. Joseph was trustworthy, and Potiphar made him responsible for his household. Then one day Potiphar's wife falsely accused Joseph of attacking her. Potiphar was furious and put him in prison. But God stayed with Joseph and helped him to interpret the dreams of the Pharaoh's baker and wine steward, who were also in prison. The dreams came true.

Two years later the Pharaoh had a strange dream, which no one could explain. Then his wine steward remembered Joseph. "Bring him here," commanded the Pharaoh.

"I cannot interpret your dream, but God will tell me its meaning," Joseph told the Pharaoh.

Joseph explained that the dream foretold seven years of good harvests followed by seven years of famine. The Pharaoh trusted Joseph and made him governor, in charge of collecting the food reserves throughout Egypt. Again, the dream came true.

When the famine reached Canaan, Jacob sent ten of his sons to Egypt to buy corn, keeping Benjamin, the youngest, at home. Joseph recognized his brothers, but they did not recognize Joseph.

JOSEPH'S JOURNEY

Joseph's brothers sold him to traders who were heading south to Egypt with spices and resins (above).

JOSEPH'S DREAM

Joseph was 17 when he dreamed his brothers bowed to him. This came true over 20 years later when he was governor of Egypt under the Pharaoh (right).

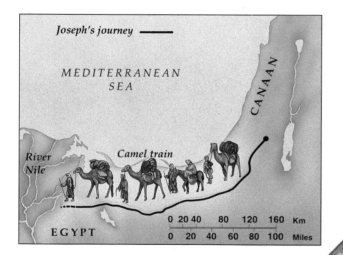

Joseph decided to test them. "You're spies," he told them. "I won't sell you any corn." The brothers protested that they were honest men, but Joseph pretended not to believe them. He insisted that they bring Benjamin to him, and kept Simeon as a hostage. The brothers returned with Benjamin, and eventually Joseph told them who he was.

Jacob was overjoyed when the brothers told him that Joseph was alive and was governor of all Egypt. "This is all I could ask for," he said. "I must go and see my son before I die."

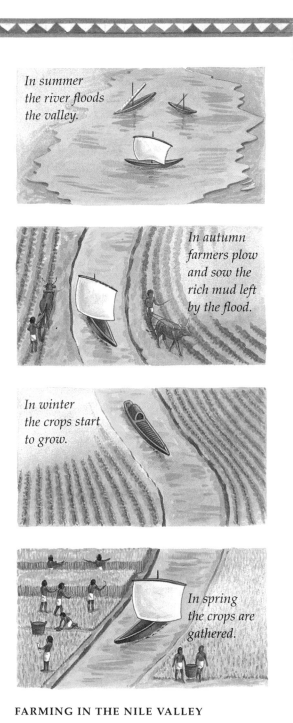

In summer the river floods the valley.

In autumn farmers plow and sow the rich mud left by the flood.

In winter the crops start to grow.

In spring the crops are gathered.

FARMING IN THE NILE VALLEY

The Nile River was vital for survival in ancient Egypt. Its annual flood, which burst the banks and covered the land with rich, fertile silt, was essential for the farmers. They cut canals and ditches to carry the water to the fields. With careful management, this enabled them to make the water last until the next flood.

MOSES: THE SLAVE WHO BECAME A PRINCE

EXODUS 1–12

JOSEPH'S FAMILY and their descendants, the Israelites, often known as Hebrews, stayed in Egypt. As their numbers grew, the Egyptians became afraid of them. A new Pharaoh forced the Hebrews to work as slaves, building the cities of Pithom and Raamses. He ordered that all Hebrew boys should be drowned in the Nile River at birth.

BRICKMAKING

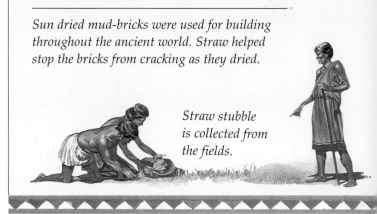

Sun dried mud-bricks were used for building throughout the ancient world. Straw helped stop the bricks from cracking as they dried.

Straw stubble is collected from the fields.

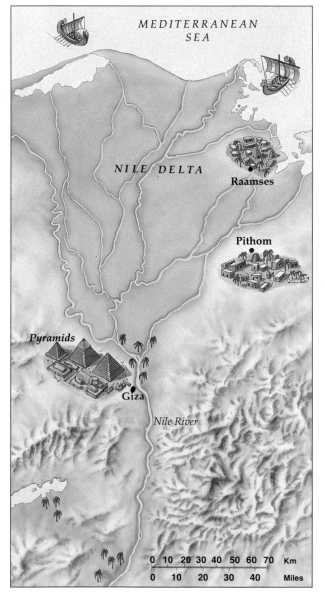

THE NILE DELTA

Every summer the Nile overflowed and left rich silt deposits on the land. Crops were harvested in spring (left).

The stubble is trampled into wet clay.

The clay mixture is put into molds to bake and harden in the sun.

After several days the hard bricks are stacked, ready for use.

One Hebrew mother saved her baby by hiding him in a basket of reeds. She covered it with tar to make it watertight and placed it among the thick reeds by the river. The Pharaoh's kind-hearted daughter found the basket when she came to the river to bathe.

"Poor baby! I shall look after him," she said. She took him to live at the Egyptian court and named him Moses.

Although Moses grew up like an Egyptian prince, he never forgot that he was a Hebrew. One day, when he was grown up, he saw an Egyptian overseer beating a Hebrew slave to make him work harder. Moses killed the Egyptian and hid his body. But the Pharaoh found out, and Moses had to flee for his life to the desert, where he became a shepherd.

Many years passed and this Pharaoh died. But the Hebrews were still slaves, and they prayed to God to rescue them.

One day Moses led his flock to pasture on Mount Sinai. There he saw a bush on fire, yet it was not burned up. As he went nearer, God spoke to him. "Moses, I am sending you back to Egypt to rescue my people."

"How can I do that?" Moses objected. "I am nobody. The Pharaoh won't listen to me."

"I will be with you," said God.

At first, the Pharaoh stubbornly refused to let the Hebrews leave, but God sent disasters on the people and their livestock as a punishment. Finally the Pharaoh gave in and agreed that the Hebrews could go.

Four hundred and thirty years after they had first settled in Egypt, the Hebrews set off on their way back to the land of Canaan, led by Moses. It was to be a long trek with deserts to cross and battles to fight with hostile tribes, but God was with them.

MOSES IN THE BASKET

The thick reeds by the Nile River were a good hiding place for the basket containing the baby Moses (left).

FORTY YEARS TO CROSS THE DESERT

EXODUS 12–40

THE ISRAELITES left Egypt in a great hurry, taking their cattle and sheep with them. They would always remember the night they left, and every year they celebrated the Passover meal as a reminder.

They started from Raamses and set out to cross the desert. The Egyptians, realizing they had lost their slaves, followed them, and the Israelites were trapped between the enemy army and the sea. But God made a dry path through the sea, and they crossed safely. The Egyptian chariots stuck in the muddy seabed, and the water rolled back and covered them.

In the desert the Israelites missed the plentiful food of Egypt and complained to Moses. But God gave them manna, which tasted like biscuits made with honey, and flocks of quail provided meat. Finding fresh water was often difficult. At one place God told Moses to strike a rock with his stick, and water came rushing out.

DRINKING WATER FOR THE ISRAELITES

There were large stretches of desert where water was scarce. At Kadesh, Moses struck a rock, and water gushed out (right).

When they reached Mount Sinai, God gave Moses the Ten Commandments and other laws and instructions about worship. God promised that he would lead the Israelites safely to the land of Canaan and settle them there if they obeyed his laws.

The people moved on in stages to the edge of the Promised Land and paused to send twelve spies ahead to see the best route and the country's defenses. The spies brought back samples of luscious fruit but reported that the cities were well fortified. "We are not strong enough to attack," said ten of the spies. Only two of them, Joshua and Caleb, spoke up bravely and said, "God is with us. We will conquer them easily." But the people refused to believe them, and God's patience was exhausted. They spent the next forty years wandering the desert until all those who had left Egypt as adults had died. Even Moses did not live to enter the land of Canaan, and it was his successor, Joshua, who led the Israelites across the Jordan River to start the conquest of the land promised to Abraham hundreds of years earlier.

FOOD IN THE DESERT

Finding fresh food in the desert often presented problems for nomads and those on the Exodus. Migrating birds, such as quail, were caught and eaten by the Israelites.

THE EXODUS

No one knows for certain the exact route of the Exodus, but this is the way they probably went southward out of Egypt and into the large desert wilderness of Sinai, then finally on to the borders of Canaan (below).

THE LAW OF THE COVENANT

After 3 months in the desert, the Israelites reached Mount Sinai. There God gave Moses the commandments and laws by which to live.

The 10 Commandments

Worship no god but me.

Do not make or worship any idols or images.

Do not use my name for any evil purpose.

Keep the Sabbath holy.

Respect your parents.

Do not murder anyone.

Do not commit adultery.

Do not steal.

Do not tell lies.

Do not long for something that belongs to someone else.

The route of the Exodus

MEDITERRANEAN SEA

Jordan River

Jericho •

CANAAN

Raamses •

Succoth •

EGYPT

Kadesh •

EDOM   MOAB

SINAI

Ezion-Geber

Mount Sinai ▲

The 10 Commandments

| 0 | 20 | 40 | 60 | 80 | 100 | 120 | Km |
| 0 | 20 | 40 | 60 | 80 | Miles |

Joshua the Great Commander

JOSHUA 6–24

To enter Canaan, the Israelites had first to take the stronghold of Jericho, with its high and strong walls. In the city people usually felt safe from attack. But this time they waited fearfully as it was the Israelite army who were outside. Everyone in Jericho had heard the stories of how God had made a path across the sea for them and how they had won battles against desert tribes.

THE ARK OF THE COVENANT

The Ark of the Covenant was a box overlaid with gold. It reminded the people of God's presence with them and contained two stone slabs on which the Ten Commandments were written.

The Israelite army leader, Joshua, organized his men. "Behind the advance guard seven priests will march, blowing trumpets. The priests carrying the Ark of the Covenant are to come next, followed by the rest of the army. You are to march round the city once in silence and come back to camp." This went on for six days.

The people of Jericho heard only the eerie sound of the ram's horn trumpets and the tramp of feet.

On the seventh day the army marched round the city seven times. Joshua ordered, "Shout! The Lord has given you the city." The soldiers roared, and the city walls collapsed. The army stormed into Jericho.

News of Joshua's victory spread through the country, and the Canaanite kings got together to fight for their territory.

Joshua knew the conquest of Canaan would be difficult, but he knew God was on Israel's side and as long as they obeyed him, the Promised Land would be theirs.

*Joshua's campaign to
capture the Promised
Land started with
attacks on towns in the
south. Then the army
headed north and
defeated the kings of the
north (below).*

**FALL OF THE CITY OF
JERICHO**

*When the walls of Jericho
collapsed, the Israelite
army went straight into
the city and destroyed it
(left). The Israelites now
had a route into Canaan.*

Joshua used siege and ambush tactics as
well as open battles in his campaign. God's
instructions were to destroy the nations of
Canaan because they were evil. The Israelites
were forbidden to mix with them or worship
their gods.

Joshua defeated thirty-one kings in his
conquest of Canaan. He divided the land
among the twelve tribes of Israel, including
Philistia, which was still unconquered.

Joshua lived to be over one hundred years
old. His last advice to the Israelites was,
"Honor God and serve him well if you want to
keep this good land he has given you."

"We will," they promised.

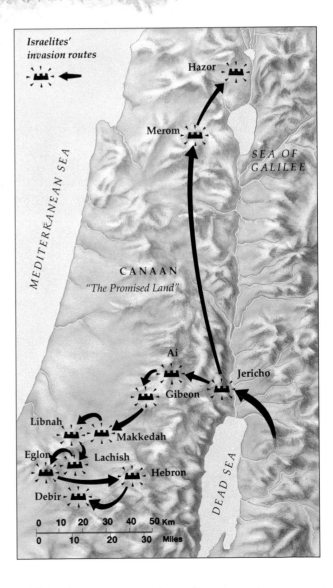

Israelites'
invasion routes

Hazor

Merom

SEA OF
GALILEE

MEDITERRANEAN SEA

CANAAN
"The Promised Land"

Ai

Jericho

Gibeon

Libnah

Makkedah

Eglon   Lachish

Debir   Hebron

DEAD SEA

| 0 | 10 | 20 | 30 | 40 | 50 Km |
| 0 | 10 | | 20 | | 30 Miles |

GIDEON: A MIGHTY HERO

JUDGES 6–16

Ａ FTER JOSHUA died, the Israelites continued to fight the Canaanites. Then, as years passed, they stopped fighting and began to mix with the peoples around them. They forgot their promise to God and started to worship the Canaanite gods. God was angry with his people and allowed other nations to take them over.

One nation, the Midianites, made surprise raids from the desert and destroyed the Israelites' crops. The Israelites were helpless against these invaders on camels and asked God for help.

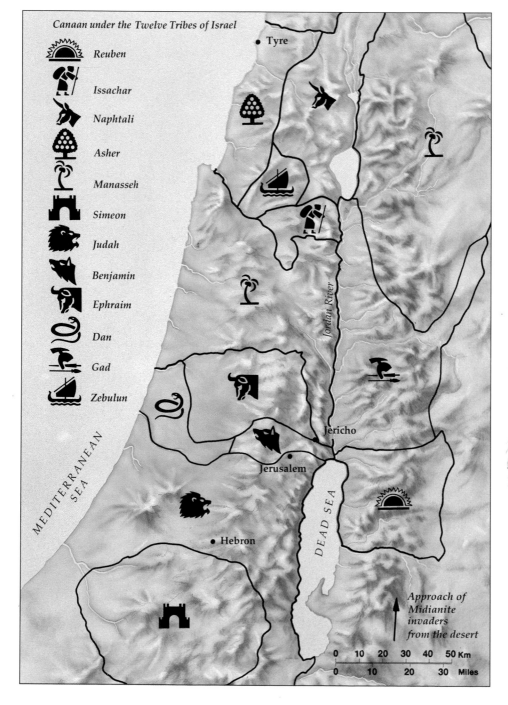

Canaan under the Twelve Tribes of Israel

Reuben
Issachar
Naphtali
Asher
Manasseh
Simeon
Judah
Benjamin
Ephraim
Dan
Gad
Zebulun

Tyre

Jordan River

Jericho

Jerusalem

Hebron

MEDITERRANEAN SEA

DEAD SEA

Approach of
Midianite
invaders
from the desert

| 0 | 10 | 20 | 30 | 40 | 50 Km |
| 0 | 10 | | 20 | | 30 Miles |

CANAAN DIVIDED

The twelve tribes of Israel were each given land in which to settle. The symbols shown were given originally by Jacob to his twelve sons (left).

One day God sent an angel to a man called Gideon. "God is sending you to rescue Israel from the Midianites," he said.

"What! How can I do that?" Gideon asked. "I'm nobody important."

"Don't be afraid. God will help you," the angel replied.

Gideon gathered an army and got ready for battle. But God told Gideon that the army was too big. He sent twenty-thousand men home and took the remaining ten thousand to a nearby stream where he watched them drink. Most of them knelt down and lapped the water like dogs. Three hundred scooped water up in their cupped hands. "Those are your men," said God. "Send the rest home."

Gideon divided his men into three groups and gave each soldier a trumpet and a jar with a torch inside it. That night they surrounded the Midianite army's camp. Then they blew the trumpets, broke the jars, and held the flaming torches high in the air, shouting, "A sword for the Lord and for Gideon." The startled Midianites woke up and found that their camp was surrounded. They began to run away, attacking one another in their confusion.

Israel won a great victory against the Midianites. In the years that followed, Samson and other leaders, called judges, carried on the struggle against nations like the Philistines. These were troubled times. The book of Judges closes with the words, "There was no king in Israel at the time. Everyone did just as he pleased."

SURPRISE ATTACK

Gideon used the cover of darkness and a clever placing of his 300 men to confuse the Midianite army and win back the Promised Land (above).

THE GODS OF THE CANAANITES

The Canaanites worshiped a number of gods and goddesses. They believed that if they did not worship them correctly, their crops would fail. They made idols and prayed to them.

Baal—the god of fertility and weather

Bronze bull— used in the worship of Baal

RUTH AND NAOMI'S TREK

RUTH 1–4

THERE WAS famine in Israel because the
crops had failed. So Naomi and
Elimelech and their two sons left their
home in Bethlehem and settled in Moab where
there was still plenty of food.

The sons grew up and married Moabite
girls, Orpah and Ruth. Then Elimelech died,
and about ten years later Naomi's sons died,
too. She was left alone, and although her
daughters-in-law were kind to her, Naomi
decided to go back to her own country where
she still had relatives.

It would be a long and lonely trek over fifty-
six miles from the mountains of Moab along
the edge of the Dead Sea and into the hilly
country round Bethlehem.

Orpah and Ruth set out with Naomi to keep
her company. After a while Naomi said to
them, "Thank you for coming so far with me.
Now go back to your own land."

The girls cried as she kissed them goodbye.
Orpah went back to Moab, but Ruth clung to

FROM CROP TO BREAD

*The sheaves of grain are
piled on the threshing
floor and trampled on by
oxen dragging a
threshing sledge. The
sledge has stones or
pieces of metal fixed to
its underside.*

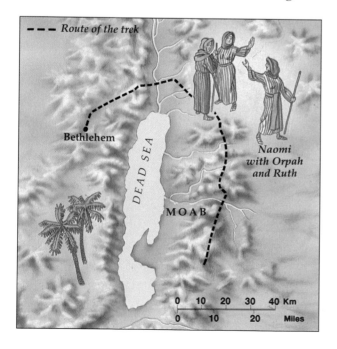

Route of the trek

Bethlehem

DEAD SEA

MOAB

*Naomi
with Orpah
and Ruth*

0   10   20   30   40 Km

0   10   20   Miles

THE JOURNEY

*Ruth and Naomi
probably walked to
Bethlehem following
tracks across the hilly
countryside (left).*

The threshed wheat is winnowed with a fork and then sifted to remove stones.

The grain is ground, using a pestle and mortar or millstones. Water and salt are mixed in to make a dough. Flat loaves of bread are baked on a metal sheet over a fire.

THE GLEANERS

Farmers were not allowed to cut corn at the edges of their fields nor go back and pick up stray ears of corn. They were left for poor people, like Ruth, to glean or gather after harvest (left).

Naomi. "Let me go with you," she pleaded. "Where you live, I will live, and your God will be my God."

So the two of them continued their journey and at last reached Bethlehem, footsore and dusty. People asked, "Is it really you, Naomi? Where's your family?"

Naomi's sad news shocked the people. They were kind to her and welcomed Ruth.

It was harvest time, and Ruth went to the fields to pick up any corn left by the harvest workers, as poor people were allowed to do. A farmer called Boaz noticed her, and when he found out who she was, he told his reapers to leave some extra corn for her. Ruth took about twenty-two pounds of grain home to Naomi that evening and ground it into flour for bread.

By the end of the harvest, Boaz had fallen in love with the girl from Moab. Naomi was delighted because he was a relative, and it was the tradition for people to marry within their tribes.

Boaz and Ruth were married. When their son, Obed, was born, Naomi loved and cared for him as though he were her own son. How glad Naomi would have been if she could have known that Obed's grandson would be David, Israel's greatest king.

SAMUEL AND SAUL: WISE AND FOOLISH LEADERS

1 SAMUEL 1–16

SAMUEL WAS only a young boy when he went to live in the temple at Shiloh. He helped Eli, the priest, with his duties. God used to talk to Samuel, and when Eli died, the people chose Samuel to be their leader, because they respected him. At this time the Philistines were at war with Israel. They held the lands along the coast, and they were fierce fighters. The Philistine warriors wore feathered headdresses, and their swords and spears were stronger and better than the Israelites' weapons.

Philistines' route with the Ark of the Covenant

PHILISTIA

MEDITERRANEAN SEA

Philistines carrying away the Ark of the Covenant

Ekron

Ashdod

Bethshemesh

Gath

Ashkelon

Gaza

PHILISTIA (PHILISTINE LANDS)

| 0 | 10 | 20 | 30 | 40 | 50 Km |
| 0 | | 5 | 10 | | 15 Miles |

Feather—topped helmet

Spear

Breastplate

Shield

A PHILISTINE WARRIOR

The Philistines were a fierce and warlike people. They had better weapons than the Israelites.

After a terrible defeat by the Philistines, the Israelites took the holy Ark of the Covenant, the symbol of God's presence, into battle, hoping they would win. But the Philistines fought even more fiercely and captured the Ark. However, disease and plague followed the Ark as the Philistines moved it from city to city, and soon they sent it back to Israel.

Samuel ruled Israel wisely, and when the people took his advice and returned to worshiping God, God helped them to defeat the Philistines.

When Samuel grew old, the leaders of the tribes came to see him. "We want a king, like the other nations. Choose a king for us."

Soon afterward, a farmer's son, named Saul, came to see Samuel to ask his help to find his father's lost donkeys. "This is the man to rule

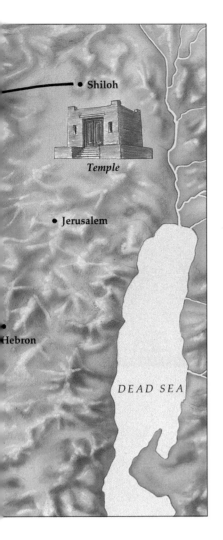

Shiloh

Temple

Jerusalem

Hebron

DEAD SEA

THE TERRITORY OF THE PHILISTINES

The Philistines made raids eastward into Israelite territory to capture more land. The name Palestine comes from the word Philistia *(left)*

my people," God told Samuel, and Samuel anointed Saul ruler of Israel.

Saul became king of Israel and led his army to victory in his first battle. But he began to ignore Samuel's advice and disobeyed God's instructions. "Because you have rejected God by disobeying him, he has rejected you as king," Samuel told Saul.

Instead, God had chosen a young shepherd boy, David, to be the next king of Israel. Samuel anointed him with oil secretly. Saul did not know. Often Saul was in despair, and his servants tried to comfort him. "Let David the shepherd play his lyre for you," and David's music soothed Saul `in his black moods. Only David and Samuel knew one day David would be king of Israel.

THE ANOINTING

Saul was anointed king by Samuel in the traditional way, using a sweet-smelling mixture of olive oil and spices. *Anointing was a sign of a king's appointment by God (above).*

DAVID: ISRAEL'S GREATEST KING

1 SAMUEL 17 AND 2 SAMUEL 5–24

DAVID WAS only a boy when he killed the Philistine giant, Goliath, with a stone hurled from his sling. The Philistines panicked when they saw their champion die, and the Israelite army won a great victory. David was a national hero, and he became close friends with Saul's son, Jonathan. Saul was so jealous of David that he tried to kill him. Once Saul tried to persuade Jonathan to kill David, but he refused. Saul was angrier than ever, and David and a band of loyal men left the city and lived in the hills while Saul and his men hunted for them.

After Saul and his sons were killed in a battle with the Philistines, David became king. At first he ruled Israel from the town of Hebron, but he needed a strong city to make his capital. One day he attacked a fortress belonging to the Jebusites. It was perched high on a rocky cliff and was well protected, but David knew there was a water tunnel under the walls. His men crawled up it and captured the fortress. David built the city of Jerusalem around the fortress and ruled his kingdom from there.

The king of Tyre sent a trade mission to David and supplied him with cedar logs, carpenters, and stonemasons to build a palace.

David had the Ark of the Covenant brought to Jerusalem, and the priests carried it in a splendid procession through the streets. Musicians played, the people sang, and even David joined in the dancing.

David still loved to play his lyre, and he wrote many songs. Many of his songs were used to lead the Israelites in worship.

David's psalms are still widely used in churches today.

DAVID'S LYRE

The instrument David played was called a kinnor. It was a lyre made of wood and sometimes decorated with ivory and silver. It was plucked with the fingers and a pick.

During David's forty years as king, he extended his kingdom as far as the border of Egypt in the south and to the Upper Euphrates in the north. The northern part was known as Israel and the southern part as Judah. David realized that God had helped him build up his strong and prosperous kingdom. When he knew he was dying, David sent for his son Solomon. "When you become king, be determined to do what God orders. If you do, God will keep his promise that my children will always rule Israel," David said.

JOYFUL PROCESSION

The Ark of the Covenant arrived in Jerusalem accompanied by music and dancing. David, too, danced for joy (above).

THE KINGDOM OF DAVID

David pushed the Philistines back toward the coast and took territory from many other tribes (right).

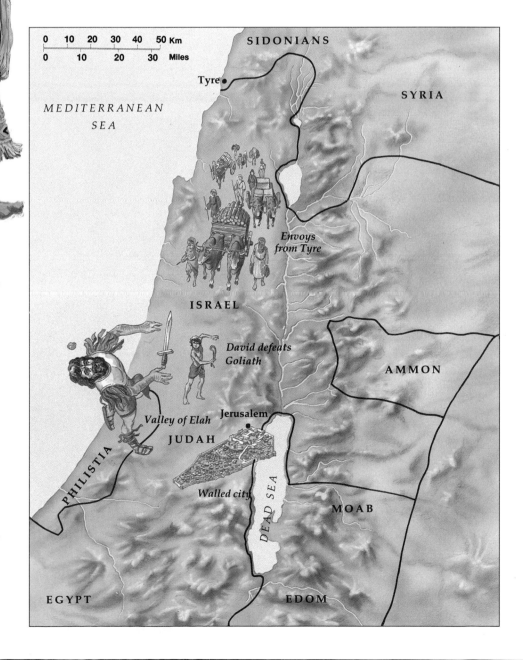

SIDONIANS

Tyre

SYRIA

MEDITERRANEAN SEA

Envoys from Tyre

ISRAEL

David defeats Goliath

AMMON

Valley of Elah Jerusalem

JUDAH

PHILISTIA

Walled city

DEAD SEA

MOAB

EGYPT

EDOM

SOLOMON'S TEMPLE

1 KINGS 3–9

SOLOMON WAS still young when he became king of Israel. One night in a dream, God asked him, "What would you like me to give you?"

"Please give me the wisdom to rule your people," Solomon answered.

Solomon's wisdom became famous, and all kinds of people asked his advice. One day two mothers came to see him. They shared the same house and had both had babies, but one baby had died in the night. One mother claimed that the other had taken her living baby and left the dead one in its place. The other woman insisted that the living baby was *hers*.

King Solomon listened to them and then sent for a sword. "Cut the living baby in two and give half to each woman," he ordered. The real mother cried, "Don't kill my baby! Give it to her."

But the other woman said "No, go ahead. Cut it in half. That's fair."

"The child belongs to the first woman," Solomon declared. He knew the real mother would want her baby to live.

Under Solomon's rule the country prospered. Soon he was able to start work on a great project—a magnificent Temple in Jerusalem where people could worship God. First he sent a request to King Hiram of Tyre, who owned the forests of Lebanon. Hiram promised to supply all the timber Solomon

THE TEMPLE

The main part was 88.5 ft long, 29.5 ft wide, and 44 ft high. It was built of stone with cedarwood (below).

THE GROWTH OF JERUSALEM

Solomon used forced labor to build the Temple and to extend Jerusalem beyond the city of David (right).

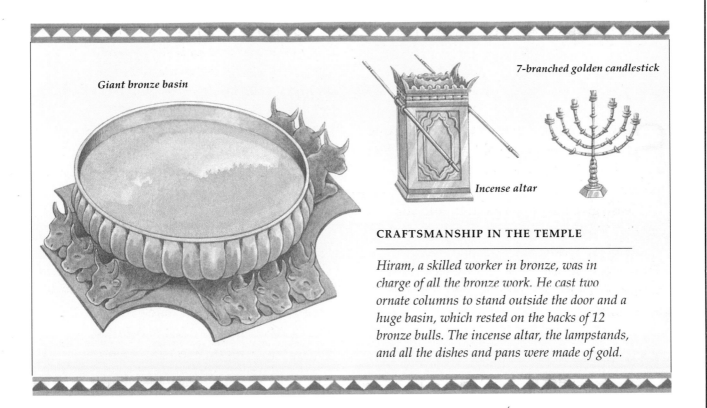

Giant bronze basin

7-branched golden candlestick

Incense altar

CRAFTSMANSHIP IN THE TEMPLE

Hiram, a skilled worker in bronze, was in charge of all the bronze work. He cast two ornate columns to stand outside the door and a huge basin, which rested on the backs of 12 bronze bulls. The incense altar, the lampstands, and all the dishes and pans were made of gold.

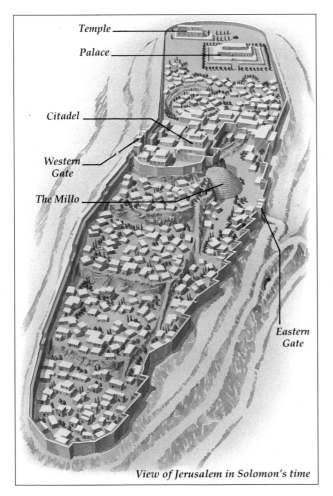

Temple

Palace

Citadel

Western Gate

The Millo

Eastern Gate

View of Jerusalem in Solomon's time

needed in return for food.

Work soon began on the Temple. The finest materials only were used. The rooms were lined with cedar panels carved with flowers, palm trees, and cherubim, and overlaid with gold. At the heart of the building was a small windowless room lined with gold to hold the Ark of the Covenant, the symbol of God's presence on Earth.

It took seven years to complete the building. King Solomon summoned all the leaders in Israel to come to Jerusalem for a special ceremony to bring the Ark of the Covenant to the Temple.

As the priests carried the Ark into the building, sacrifices were offered to thank God. When the Ark had been placed in the inner room and the priests were leaving, the Lord's presence filled the Temple.

Solomon knelt in worship and prayed, "Lord God of Israel, watch over this temple where you have chosen to be worshiped and hear my prayers and the prayers of my people."

Cargoes of Ivory, Gold, and Monkeys

1 KINGS 10–11

King Solomon took full advantage of the trade routes that ran through Israel. He became very rich because of this trade. He would buy horses in Turkey and sell them to the Egyptians. From the Egyptians he bought chariots, which he sold to other countries.

Solomon also had a fleet of ships built at Ezion-Geber. He hired skilled Phoenician seamen to help train the less experienced Israelite sailors. They sailed to Ophir and brought back rich cargoes of gold, silver, copper, ivory, juniper wood, and monkeys.

Solomon's palace was decorated with gold, and his throne was the grandest at that time. It was covered in ivory and gold and had six steps leading up to it with carved lions at the end of each step and beside the two arms.

A PHOENICIAN GALLEY

The Phoenicians were skillful sailors, shipbuilders, and sea traders. Solomon hired them for his trade in boats such as this, which sailed westward along the Mediterranean and into the Atlantic.

The fame of Solomon's wealth and wisdom spread, and people traveled from far and wide to trade with him and to listen to him. Traders and merchants brought him gifts and enjoyed his generous hospitality.

The Queen of Sheba came from Arabia with many servants and a camel train laden with jewels, gold, and spices to trade with Solomon. As well as trade with his country, the Queen also wanted to test his wisdom, so she asked him difficult questions. Solomon answered them all, and the Queen of Sheba was amazed.

He showed her around his richly decorated palace and the vast stables for his chariot and cavalry horses. She saw the huge amounts of beef, lamb, venison, and fowl prepared in his kitchens and served on dishes of gold. She also visited the magnificent Temple.

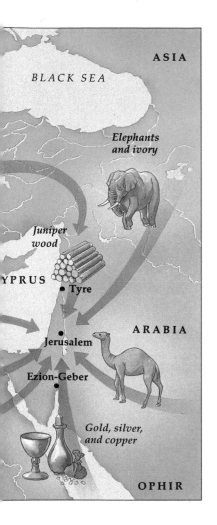

ASIA

BLACK SEA

Elephants and ivory

Juniper wood

YPRUS

● Tyre

ARABIA

Jerusalem

● Ezion-Geber

Gold, silver, and copper

OPHIR

THE VISIT OF THE QUEEN OF SHEBA

The Queen of Sheba wanted trade with Solomon, and to see if the fame of his wisdom was true. She presented many gifts to him at his grand palace (right).

TRADE ROUTES

An ancient north-south trade route ran along Israel's coast. Solomon increased the nation's trade with Egypt and Arabia to the south, and the Mediterranean lands to the north (above).

Impressed, the Queen said, "What I heard about you is true. Indeed, I didn't hear even half of it! Your wisdom and wealth are breathtaking." She returned to Arabia, leaving Solomon a gift of all she had brought.

Solomon recognized the importance of strong trade links and did all he could to encourage them. He married an Egyptian princess to strengthen these links with Egypt and went on to marry other foreign women, many of whom did not worship the God of Israel. Solomon loved all his wives dearly, but he let them build shrines to their own gods and began to join his wives in their worship. God was angry with Solomon because he had broken his promise to love and obey him. God warned him that he would tear the kingdom away from Solomon's son.

DIVIDED LOYALTIES: GOD OR BAAL?

1 KINGS 12–18

KING SOLOMON had a son called Rehoboam, who became the next king of Israel. Like his father, he asked for advice about how to rule, but he did not ask God, as Solomon had done. Instead he consulted King Solomon's old advisers, who told him to treat people fairly and they would be loyal. He ignored their advice and listened instead to his foolish young friends, who urged him to be a hard ruler.

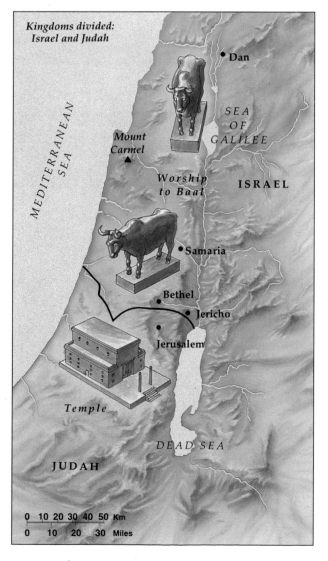

Kingdoms divided: Israel and Judah

- Dan
- SEA OF GALILEE
- Mount Carmel
- Worship to Baal
- ISRAEL
- MEDITERRANEAN SEA
- Samaria
- Bethel
- Jericho
- Jerusalem
- Temple
- DEAD SEA
- JUDAH

0 10 20 30 40 50 Km
0   10   20   30 Miles

As a result, the nation divided, and only two tribes stayed loyal to Rehoboam. They became the kingdom of Judah. The remaining ten tribes formed the northern kingdom of Israel under a new king, Jeroboam.

Jeroboam did not want his people to travel to God's Temple in Jerusalem in Judah. Instead he set up two gold statues of calves in his own territory. "People of Israel, here are your gods," he said. So the people of Israel disobeyed God and began to pray to these statues and to other pagan gods.

As the years passed, one bad king followed another, and worship of God was almost forgotten. By the time of King Ahab, the people had started worshiping the god Baal. Ahab's wife, Jezebel, believed Baal controlled the weather. God decided it was time to speak to Ahab.

One day a man called Elijah appeared at Ahab's palace with a message from God. He told Ahab that God, not Baal, was in control of the weather and there would be no more rain until God said so.

Elijah had to go into hiding because Ahab and Jezebel were so angry that they tried to kill him. During the drought that followed, God protected Elijah and provided food for him. Three years later when the rivers were dry and the land parched, God said to Elijah, "Go and tell Ahab that I will send rain."

Elijah told Ahab to summon the priests of Baal and all the people to the slopes of Mount Carmel to test who was the real god. The priests built an altar to Baal, piled firewood on it, and placed a bull on top as a sacrifice. "Now ask Baal to send fire to burn the

DIVIDED KINGDOM

Samaria became the capital of the northern kingdom, Israel, The temple in Jerusalem belonged to Judah (left).

CONTEST ON MOUNT CARMEL

Elijah called to God, and fire burned his sacrifice and also the altar. The priests, people, and King Ahab (in his chariot), who worshiped Baal, were frightened by this dramatic challenge to their god (below).

MAKING A SACRIFICE

The Israelites had strict laws about sacrifices. The basic idea was that the sin of the person was placed on the animal, which was then killed. But the Canaanite religion involved sacrifices of children.

sacrifice," Elijah challenged. All day the priests prayed to Baal, and nothing happened. Then Elijah built his altar and even poured water on the firewood. "O Lord, prove now that you are the God of Israel," he prayed. At once flames spurted around the sacrifice. The people fell to the ground exclaiming, "The Lord alone is God!"

Jonah, the Reluctant Prophet

JONAH 1–4

ELIJAH WAS just one of many prophets sent by God to speak to his people. The prophets not only foretold future events but they also spoke to remind the nation and its leaders of how God had helped them in the past.

ASSYRIAN LION HUNT

The King of Assyria hunted lions with his servants, firing arrows from his chariot. This drawing is based on a carving originally from the royal palace at Nineveh, the capital of the Assyrian empire.

They encouraged the people to live as God wanted them to and warned them of God's displeasure when they disobeyed him. Prophets who spoke God's word fearlessly were not always popular, and it was not an easy or safe life.

God spoke one day to a prophet named Jonah. "Go to Nineveh," he told him, "and warn the people about their wickedness."

Nineveh was the capital city of Assyria, Israel's enemy. Jonah's response was to head in the opposite direction. He went to the port of Joppa and boarded a ship bound for Spain. Jonah's efforts to run away were thwarted when God sent a violent storm, and the ship was in danger of breaking up. The crew threw the cargo overboard to lighten the ship. The captain discovered Jonah asleep in the hold and woke him, urging him to pray for help. Jonah admitted that he was the cause of the storm because he was running away from God. "Throw me overboard and it will become calm," he said. The sailors were reluctant to do this, but as the storm grew worse, they did as Jonah said. Jonah disappeared into the raging waters, the sea grew calm, and the awestruck sailors vowed to follow God. Jonah did not drown but was swallowed alive by a huge fish sent by God. From inside the fish Jonah prayed to God. Three days later the fish ejected Jonah from its mouth onto a beach. This time when God said "Go to Nineveh," Jonah went!

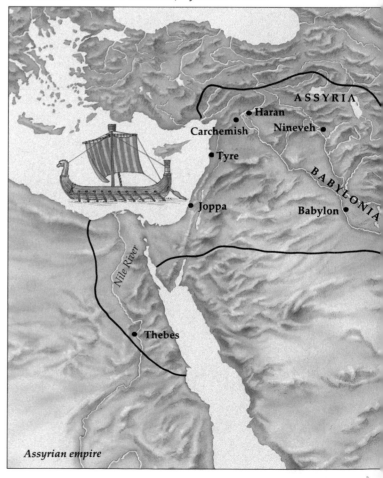

Assyrian empire

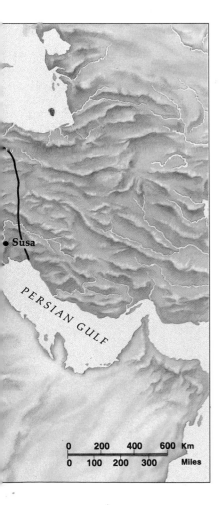

OVERBOARD!

Sailors threw the prophet Jonah into the stormy sea as he had asked them to do, because Jonah believed God was angry with him and this act would save the ship (above).

ASSYRIAN EMPIRE

The Assyrians pushed their borders south into Egypt, west into the Mediterranean, north into Asia Minor, and east into the Persian Gulf (left).

The people of Nineveh listened to Jonah and believed that God would destroy their city if they did not change. From the king of Assyria downward, they declared their intention to give up their evil and violent ways. God relented and did not punish them.

But instead of being pleased, Jonah was angry, because he did not care for the Assyrians and God had shown mercy to them.

Jonah still had to learn that God's forgiveness was offered to all and not just to his own people.

War and Exile

2 KINGS 17, 18, AND 25

At the time when Israel and Judah became two separate kingdoms, the powerful Assyrian empire was growing in the east.

The Assyrians were ruthless fighters, and their cruelty in warfare made them much feared. They threatened Israel in the time of Ahab, but he made an alliance with the king of Syria and halted their advance for a time. The Assyrians were still a threat to Israel, and the prophets of God warned the Israelites that if they continued to break God's laws and worship other gods, God would not save them from the Assyrians. The people ignored the warnings and continued to follow the customs of the surrounding nations, even sacrificing children to pagan gods.

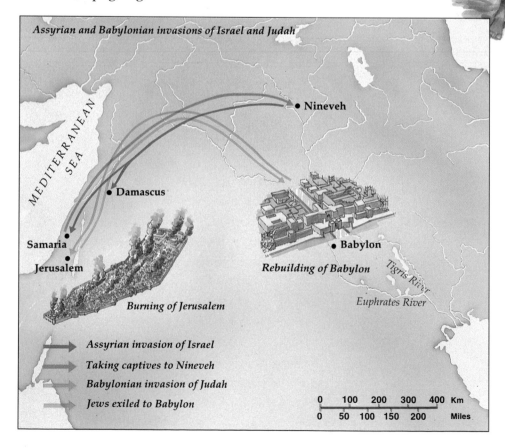

Assyrian and Babylonian invasions of Israel and Judah

MEDITERRANEAN SEA

Nineveh

Damascus

Samaria

Jerusalem

Burning of Jerusalem

Rebuilding of Babylon

Babylon

Tigris River

Euphrates River

→ Assyrian invasion of Israel
→ Taking captives to Nineveh
→ Babylonian invasion of Judah
→ Jews exiled to Babylon

| 0 | 100 | 200 | 300 | 400 | Km |
| 0 | 50 | 100 | 150 | 200 | Miles |

ASSYRIAN ATTACKS

Siege engines with ramps were made of wood and covered with animal skin. Assyrian soldiers pushed them right up to the city walls. The cover gave some protection to archers inside (above).

EXILED JEWS

The Assyrians captured Samaria, capital of Israel, in 722 B.C. and exiled the Jews to all parts of their empire. The Babylonians destroyed Jerusalem in 586 B.C. and also took the Jews into exile (left).

In the end God allowed the Assyrians to overrun Israel, and the ten tribes were taken into captivity in Assyria. They never returned to their own land.

The kingdom of Judah stayed faithful to God for a time, but the people there also gave up worshiping God. Prophets like Micah and Jeremiah warned that God would abandon Judah also to their enemies. King Sennacherib of Assyria attacked the fortified cities of Judah and conquered them, but Jerusalem survived.

By the end of the seventh century B.C. the Assyrian empire stretched from the Tigris River to the Nile River.

In the following century the Babylonians defeated the Assyrians. The conquering king, Nebuchadnezzar, rebuilt the city of Babylon in magnificent style. He proceeded to establish his own empire. First he defeated Egypt, and then he invaded Judah. He attacked Jerusalem, taking the king of Judah and ten thousand prisoners back to Babylon. Nebuchadnezzar also plundered the Temple and broke up all the gold utensils that Solomon had made. Only the poorest and unskilled people were left in Judah, and a king called Zedekiah was appointed to rule them.

When Zedekiah rebelled against Babylonian rule, King Nebuchadnezzar returned with all his army and besieged Jerusalem. The siege lasted for eighteen months, and there was no food left in the city by the time the Babylonians breached the walls.

King Nebuchadnezzar's army burned the Temple, the palace, and all the important buildings and tore down the city walls. They carried away all the people into exile, leaving only the poorest people to work in the fields and vineyards.

Many of the exiles never saw their Judean homeland again, for it was seventy years before Cyrus the Great, who defeated the Babylonians, allowed the Jews to return.

SIEGE MACHINES

The Assyrians were skilled in siege warfare. They built mounds and ramps to roll their battering rams as near to the top of Israelite city walls as possible.

DANIEL, GOD'S FAITHFUL SERVANT

DANIEL 1, 2 AND 6

THE JEWISH exiles in Babylon thought sadly of their homeland far away.

"By the waters of Babylon,
there we sat down and wept
when we remembered Zion.
On the willows there we hung
up our lyres.
How shall we sing the Lord's song in
a foreign land?"

They tried to worship God, but it was not easy in a land where the people spoke a different language and had many false gods. But some were determined to stay loyal to the one true God, whatever the cost.

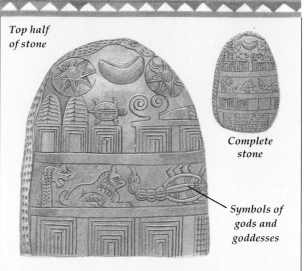

Top half of stone

Complete stone

Symbols of gods and goddesses

BABYLONIAN BOUNDARY STONES

The Babylonians used boundary stones in fields or by temples to mark out the ownership of land. The carvings on the stone included symbols of the gods and goddesses as witnesses to the land claims.

CITY OF BABYLON

Close-up of Babylon, the capital richly restored by Nebuchadnezzar. Many Jewish exiles would have passed through the main gate (below).

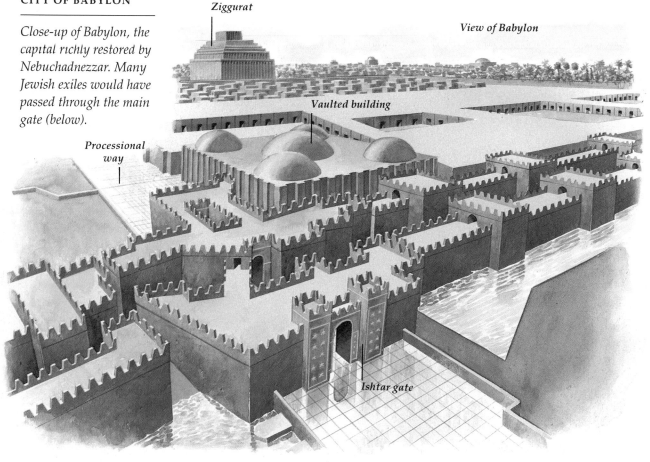

Ziggurat

View of Babylon

Vaulted building

Processional way

Ishtar gate

King Nebuchadnezzar gave orders that some of the young Jewish prisoners should be trained to serve him at court. Among those chosen were Daniel and his three friends, Shadrach, Meshach, and Abednego. At the start of their training, they told the official in charge, "We cannot eat Babylonian food, because our God has given us rules about the kinds of food we may eat." The official was fearful of trouble if Daniel and his friends looked unhealthy, but he soon discovered that their vegetarian diet made them fitter than the others.

Soon afterward King Nebuchadnezzar had a dream, which worried him. He sent for his magicians. "You must tell me both the dream and its meaning," he insisted, "or else I'll have you put to death."

Daniel heard the news, and he and his three friends met to pray. That night God showed Daniel the dream and its meaning.

Daniel went to King Nebuchadnezzar. "In your dream you saw a huge statue made of gold, silver, iron, and clay. Suddenly a great stone fell on the statue and smashed it. Then the stone grew into a huge mountain filling the earth." Daniel continued, "God is showing you that one day your empire will be destroyed, but God will set up his own kingdom that will last forever."

DANIEL IN THE PIT

Thrown into a pit of lions by his Babylonian masters as punishment for praying to God, Daniel was not harmed by the lions because God protected him (above).

King Nebuchadnezzar was very impressed and made Daniel his chief adviser. Daniel thanked God and continued to worship him.

Daniel lived through the reign of King Nebuchadnezzar and his son. He was an old man when King Darius the Mede seized power. He made Daniel one of his chief officials, but jealous men plotted to remove Daniel. They persuaded King Darius to make a law forbidding prayer to any God for a month. Anyone who ignored this law was to be thrown into a pit of lions. Daniel continued to pray to God as before, and he was flung into the pit. But God shut the lions' mouths, and Daniel's life was saved.

God still had work for his faithful servant in the land of exile.

NEHEMIAH REBUILDS JERUSALEM

NEHEMIAH 1–12

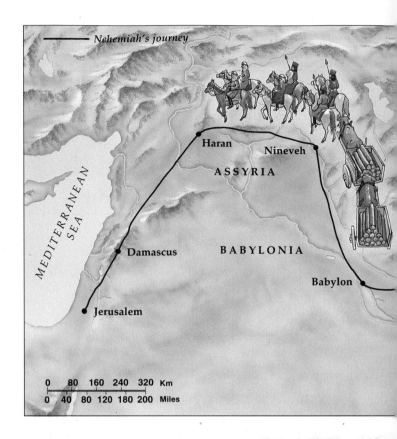

Nehemiah's journey

MEDITERRANEAN SEA

ASSYRIA

BABYLONIA

Haran · Nineveh · Damascus · Babylon · Jerusalem

| 0 | 80 | 160 | 240 | 320 | Km |
| 0 | 40 | 80 | 120 | 180 | 200 | Miles |

THE MIGHTY Babylonian empire was conquered by the Persians, whose king generously allowed the Jews to return to their own land. Many of them left Babylon and traveled back to settle in their old towns. They started to rebuild the Temple in Jerusalem, but difficulties held up the work.

Some Jews stayed in exile. One of these was Nehemiah, who was wine steward to the Persian king, Artaxerxes. One day the king asked him, "Why are you so sad, Nehemiah?"

"Your Majesty, I have news from Jerusalem that the city is still in ruins. The people have lost heart and stopped rebuilding," Nehemiah replied. "And what do you want from me?" inquired Artaxerxes.

Nehemiah prayed silently to God for help before he answered the king. He asked for permission to go back to rebuild Jerusalem, and the king agreed. He also gave Nehemiah permits to travel across his empire and promised him timber for building.

When Nehemiah arrived in Jerusalem, he rode around the city at night on a donkey to see for himself what needed to be done. Next morning he met the leaders of the town and told them his plans. He encouraged them to start work, and soon almost everyone in Jerusalem wanted to join in.

Nehemiah organized the rebuilding of the walls and gave people responsibility for short sections near their homes. At first all went well, but some of the foreigners who had settled in the area resented the rebuilding and threatened to stop it.

Nehemiah reassured the fearful Jews. "Remember that God is with us. He will defeat their plans."

MISSION TO REBUILD

Nehemiah traveled about 800 miles across mountains and desert and through the province of West Euphrates to help rebuild Jerusalem (left).

WALLS REBUILT

Nehemiah and his bugler kept watch as the walls of Jerusalem were restored. Soldiers, too, stood on guard against possible attacks (below).

FESTIVAL OF SHELTERS

The Jewish priest, Ezra, encouraged people to keep old festivals forgotten by the Jews in exile. The Festival of Shelters remembered those who had first trekked across the desert to the Promised Land. Branches were made into shelters on flat-roofed homes. People sang and danced for a week.

Nehemiah placed sentries along the wall to guard it night and day. He also gave the builders weapons in case of attack. As Nehemiah walked around supervising the work, he was accompanied by a bugler ready to sound the alarm. Nehemiah's enthusiasm spurred the people, and they worked eagerly and completed the walls, over a mile long, in just seven weeks. At the ceremony to dedicate the city walls to God, singers and musicians led a triumphant procession along the top of the walls.

A priest called Ezra, who had also returned from exile, helped the people to start worship in the Temple when the rebuilding was completed. Ezra gathered all the people together in a city square and read to them from the book of the law, which God had given Moses. The people were upset when they realized that they had not been faithful to God. They signed an agreement that from then on, they would keep the law and not neglect going to the Temple to worship God.

LOOKING BACKWARD AND FORWARD

THE SMALL country of Israel was in the center of the civilized world and was invaded and occupied by successive empires: first, the Assyrians and later the Babylonians in 586 B.C.

About fifty years later, King Cyrus of Persia defeated the Babylonians and began to build the vast Persian empire. Under Persian rule the exiled Jews were allowed to return home, and they began to restore their nation and also started to build local places of worship called synagogues.

The exiled Jews collected the stories of Israel's history, the laws God had given Moses, and the poetry and writings of David and Solomon, and these were later included in the Hebrew Bible. Teachers of the law, called rabbis, explained the Bible.

Prophets, inspired by God, told the people how they should live their lives. Through the prophets God told the Jews that one day he would send them a special Savior King. These stories are covered in the first part of the Bible, the Old Testament.

Hundreds of years were to pass before the prophesies were fulfilled in the birth of Jesus. During that time Palestine became part of two more empires: the Greek, then the Roman.

Alexander the Great was only twenty-one when he set out from Greece, in the fourth century B.C., to march east with his armies and conquer the Persian empire, which included the land of Palestine.

BETWEEN THE TESTAMENTS

For the next two hundred years, Greek ways of living influenced the Jews in Palestine. This period of history falls between the Old Testament and the New Testament.

After Alexander's death, rival Greek rulers fought for control of Palestine. One of these rulers, Antiochus Epiphanes, tried to wipe out the Jewish religion. The Jews rebelled and set up their own kings for a time until the Romans conquered Palestine in 63 B.C. The Roman empire was the setting for the world into which Jesus was born. His story is told in the second part of the Bible, the New Testament.

THE WORLD OF THE NEW TESTAMENT

The Romans brought thousands of soldiers into Palestine to keep the Jews under control. The Jews were forced to pay heavy taxes and were expected to worship the emperor. They refused because they worshiped God alone.

The Jews longed for the coming of the Messiah, the Savior, promised by the prophets, believing that he would be their king and set them free from hated rulers. When Jesus came, many were disappointed because he was not the type of leader they had expected. "My kingdom is not of this world," Jesus said.

Bible Timelines

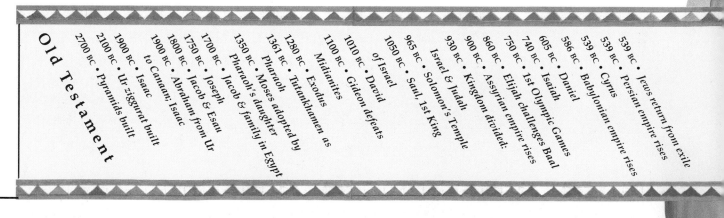

Old Testament

2700 BC • Pyramids built
2100 BC • Ur Ziggurat built
1900 BC • Isaac
1900 BC • Abraham from Ur to Canaan; Isaac
1800 BC • Jacob & Esau
1750 BC • Joseph
1700 BC • Jacob & family in Egypt
1350 BC • Pharaoh's daughter
1361 BC • Pharaoh Tutankhamen as
1280 BC • Moses adopted by
1100 BC • Exodus
1100 BC • Midianites
1010 BC • Gideon defeats
1050 BC • David of Israel
965 BC • Saul, 1st King
930 BC • Solomon's King
900 BC • Israel & Judah
860 BC • Solomon's Temple
750 BC • Kingdom divided:
740 BC • Assyrian empire rises
605 BC • Elijah challenges Baal
586 BC • 1st Olympic Games
539 BC • Isaiah
539 BC • Daniel
539 BC • Cyrus
539 BC • Babylonian empire rises
539 BC • Persian empire rises
539 BC • Jews return from exile

After Jesus had died and risen to life, his followers went everywhere telling people that he was the Savior and that through his death their sins would be forgiven and their lives changed. They spread the gospel.

Christianity was seen as a new religion, so the Romans imprisoned Christians, and many were put to death for refusing to worship the emperor. It was almost three hundred years before Christianity became an accepted religion under the emperor, Constantine.

ALEXANDER'S INVASIONS

Alexander the Great's 12-year campaign from 334–323 B.C. destroyed the Persian empire that had started over 200 years earlier in 539 B.C. Alexander pushed his empire as far east as the borders of India. The port of Alexandria in Egypt was built in his honor. He died in Babylon at the young age of 33 (below).

ARAL SEA

Oxus River

Route of Alexander's campaigns

BLACK SEA

CASPIAN SEA

Bactra

Bucephala

Nisibis

Issus

Ninus

Pella

GREECE

Arbela

Ecbatana

INDIA

Thapsacus

PERSIA

Phra

Athens

Tyre

Babylon

Susa

Persepolis

Indus River

Jerusalem

Pura

JUDAH

PERSIAN GULF

Alexandria

EGYPT

Memphis

ARABIA

MEDITERRANEAN SEA

Between the Testaments

500 BC • Persian empire & Palestine

334-323 BC • Alexander the Great's campaigns

275 BC • Old Testament translated into Greek

63 BC • Romans conquer Palestine

63 BC • Jesus under Roman control

44 BC • Julius Caesar murdered

37 BC • Herod rules Palestine

27 BC-AD 14 • Caesar Augustus, 1st Roman emperor

New Testament

4 BC • Birth of Jesus

10 BC-0 • John the Baptist

4 BC-AD 33 • Life of Jesus

AD 34/35 • Conversion of Paul

AD 46-62 • Paul's missionary adventures

AD 41-54 • Emperor Claudius

AD 54-68 • Emperor Nero

AD 81-96 • Persecution of Christians

AD 312 • Constantine accepts Christianity

Nile River

RED SEA

INDIAN OCEAN

THE SAVIOR BORN IN A STABLE

MATTHEW 2, LUKE 2

THE ROMANS were the new masters of the world. Their armies marched west across Europe and invaded Britain under Julius Caesar. One of his generals, Pompey, conquered Palestine in 63 B.C. and brought the country into the Roman empire. The Romans kept the local king, Herod, in power as their friend and ally.

During Herod's reign, Jesus was born. While his mother, Mary, was expecting him, she had to travel with her husband, Joseph, from Nazareth in the north of Israel to Bethlehem in the south as part of a Roman check on population numbers to see who should pay taxes. Everyone had to go to his hometown, and Joseph's family came from Bethlehem.

When Joseph and Mary arrived in Bethlehem, they found the town packed with people who had come to register. The inn was full, and they had to spend the night in the stable. There Jesus was born, and Mary wrapped the baby in the customary strips of cloth and laid him to sleep in the manger on top of the hay.

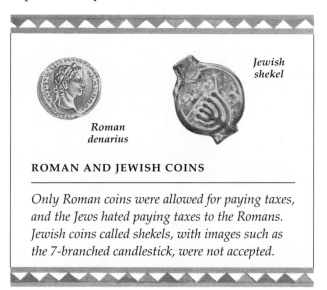

Jewish shekel

Roman denarius

ROMAN AND JEWISH COINS

Only Roman coins were allowed for paying taxes, and the Jews hated paying taxes to the Romans. Jewish coins called shekels, with images such as the 7-branched candlestick, were not accepted.

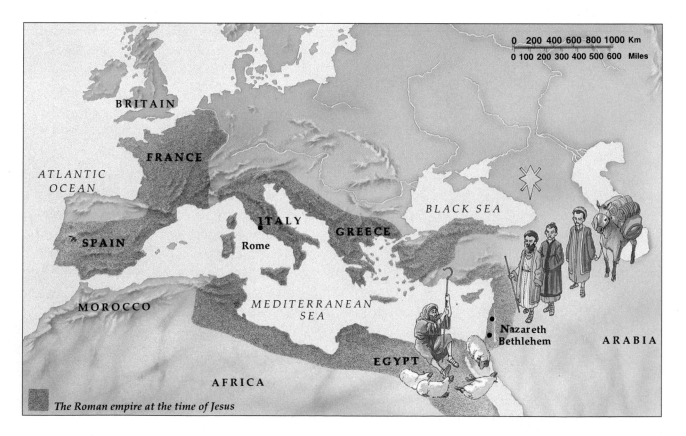

The Roman empire at the time of Jesus

THE ROMAN EMPIRE

The Romans ruled a vast empire, stretching from Britain to Egypt, and from Morocco to the Black Sea (left).

LYING IN A MANGER

After the shepherds visited Jesus, they told everyone the amazing story about the angels and the baby (above).

That night shepherds guarding their flocks in the fields outside Bethlehem were startled by the appearance of an angel announcing, "Good News! Today a Savior has been born to you—Christ the Lord!" Hundreds of angels joined him, singing "Glory to God in the highest, and peace on earth to those with whom he is pleased."

The angel told the shepherds to look in the stable, and they rushed to the town and found Mary and Joseph and the baby, just as the angel had said.

Some time later wise men arrived from the east at King Herod's palace in Jerusalem and asked, "Where is the baby born to be king of the Jews? We saw his star in the east and have come to worship him."

Herod was furious and jealous. He was the king, and he didn't want a rival. He spoke to the Jewish teachers. "The prophets have said that the Messiah will be born in Bethlehem," they told him. Herod sent the wise men to Bethlehem and told them to report back to him. He pretended that he wanted to go and worship the new king, too.

The wise men found the baby Jesus and gave him rich gifts of gold, frankincense, and myrrh, but they did not go back to Herod because God warned them not to in a dream.

Herod was furious at being outwitted and gave orders that all baby boys in the Bethlehem area should be killed.

An angel appeared to Joseph in a dream and warned him about Herod's wicked plan. Joseph decided to take Mary and the baby Jesus to Egypt where they stayed until Herod died. Then they returned to Nazareth where Jesus grew up, helping his father Joseph in the carpenter's shop.

John the Baptist prepares for Jesus

LUKE 1, 3; MARK 6

DURING THE reign of King Herod, there was a priest named Zechariah, who worked in the Temple in Jerusalem. One day, as he stood at the altar, the angel Gabriel appeared and told him that his wife, Elizabeth, would have a son. Zechariah could not believe it, because both he and his wife were old.

Because of Zechariah's disbelief, the angel said he would not be able to speak until the baby was born. Gabriel also said that the baby should be named John and that he would grow up to be a great man of God who would prepare the way for the Lord.

When a baby boy was born to Elizabeth, everyone wanted to name him after his father. Zechariah shook his head and wrote on a writing tablet: "His name is John."

Suddenly Zechariah could speak again. The neighbors were alarmed at these events, and word got around that John was a special child.

ANCIENT WRITING TABLETS

Wooden writing tablets were like shallow boxes with wax in the bottom and were written on with a stylus. The writing could be smoothed over and the tablet used again. They were common in Roman schools.

When he grew up, John lived alone in the desert. He wore a tunic of camel's hair cloth and ate locusts and wild honey. God spoke to him and sent him to preach by the Jordan River. He urged people to turn away from their sins, and he baptized them in the river as a sign that they had been forgiven.

Crowds came to hear John and be baptized. People wondered if he was the Messiah, but John said that he was preparing the way for someone greater. "I am not good enough even to untie his sandals," he said. "He will baptize you with the Holy Spirit."

One day Jesus arrived at the Jordan River and was baptized by John. As Jesus came up out of the water, the Holy Spirit came in the form of a dove and landed on him. A voice spoke from heaven. "You are my own dear Son. I am pleased with you."

BAPTISM OF JESUS

John preached in the Jordan Valley and baptized Jesus in the Jordan River at Bethabara (below).

THE LAND OF JORDAN

The Jordan River winds through wheat fields overlooked by steep, barren hillsides. Nazareth is in open hill country (right).

The lands where Jesus grew up

0 10 20 30 Km
0 5 10 15 Miles

SEA OF GALILEE

Nazareth

JORDAN RIVER VALLEY

John preaching to the crowds

Jordan River

Wilderness of Judea

Jericho

Bethabara

AMMON

Jerusalem

Fortress

JUDAH

Machaerus

DEAD SEA

MOAB

John preached to everyone and was not even afraid to tell King Herod that he had done wrong in marrying Herodias, his brother's wife. Herod responded by imprisoning John in the gloomy fortress of Machaerus. Herodias wanted John killed, but Herod did not harm him because he was afraid of offending the Jews who considered John to be a prophet.

On Herod's birthday the daughter of Herodias danced at the feast. Herod was so pleased that he offered her anything she wanted. "Ask for the head of John the Baptist," Herodias said, seizing her chance.

The king was sorry, but he would not go back on his foolish promise, and John was beheaded. When Jesus heard the sad news, he went away to a lonely place by himself.

Jesus at Work in Galilee

MARK 1, 2, 6; JOHN 2

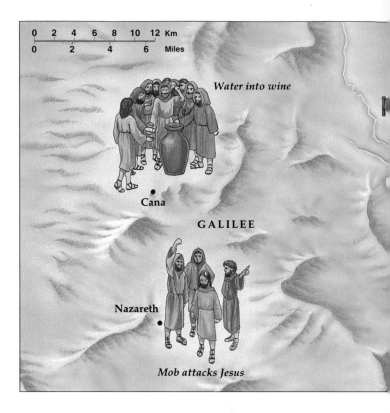

ONE DAY as Jesus was walking along the shore by the Sea of Galilee, he saw two brothers, Simon and Andrew, catching fish with a net.

Jesus called to them, "Come with me and I will teach you to catch men." At once they left their fishing and went with Jesus. Further along the beach two other brothers, James and John, were in their boat getting their nets ready. Jesus called them and they came, too. Some days later Jesus called other men to follow him until he had a group of twelve friends. These men, known as his disciples, traveled around with Jesus, helped him in his ministry, and listened to his teaching. Two of the disciples, Matthew and John, later wrote their stories of Jesus' life in the New Testament gospels.

Jesus and his disciples walked the roads to the towns and villages in the hills around Galilee, teaching people about God's love and forgiveness. Nazareth, his hometown, was the only place where Jesus was not warmly welcomed.

Once Jesus was invited to a wedding in the village of Cana. In those days wedding celebrations lasted for several days. During the feasting the wine ran out. Jesus amazed everyone by changing water into wine, and the feast went on.

Simon and Andrew came from Capernaum on the Sea of Galilee's north shore. Jesus visited their home one day and was told that Simon's mother-in-law was in bed with fever. Jesus cured the fever. Word got around, and soon the street outside was full of sick people asking Jesus to heal them.

JESUS' MIRACLES

Jesus was brought up in Nazareth, home of Joseph and Mary, and it was from there, by the Sea of Galilee, that he began his ministry (above).

Healing miracles

Bethsaida

Capernaum

Jesus works wonders

SEA OF
GALILEE

Jordan River

HOUSES IN THE TIME OF JESUS

Small, with few windows, most houses had only one floor, but there was an outside staircase to the roof, which became an extra room.

Flat roof of brushwood overlaid with clay

Outside staircase

Animals sheltered in lower area

A few days later Jesus was teaching in another house when four men arrived, carrying their paralyzed friend. They could not get near Jesus for the crowds of people, but they carried the man up the outside staircase onto the flat roof. They made a hole in the roof and lowered him down into the room where Jesus was, so that he could heal him.

Soon there were so many people wanting to see Jesus that he began to teach outside by the Sea of Galilee. Jesus would sit in a boat in the shallow water while the people crowded around the water's edge. He told them stories to explain his teaching, and the people loved to listen to him.

One day Jesus and his disciples set off for a quiet place near Bethsaida for a rest. But still crowds followed them, and Jesus did not have the heart to send them away. He talked on into the evening until his disciples pointed out that everyone was hungry. A boy offered them five small loaves and two fish. Jesus thanked God for the food, and the disciples began to hand it out. And there was plenty for all that crowd of five thousand people!

Through miracles like these, many people understood that Jesus was someone very special.

CALL TO THE DISCIPLES

Jesus summoned James and John to travel with him and be his helpers. Simon and Andrew had already joined him as disciples (left).

A WARM WELCOME AT JERUSALEM

LUKE 6, 10, 19

THE TIME came for Jesus to leave Galilee and head south to Jerusalem, the capital city.

Wherever he went, his disciples came, too, and Jesus was always teaching them about God so that they, in turn, could spread the good news to others.

There were also other teachers who did not like Jesus or his teachings. They often asked him difficult questions to try to trick him. One day a lawyer said to Jesus, "God says I should love my neighbor as myself, but who is my neighbor?" Jesus answered him by telling a story about a traveler who set out from Jerusalem down the lonely road to Jericho. Robbers attacked him and beat him up. As the injured man lay by the roadside, two men from the Temple came along, but they ignored him. It was a Samaritan, looked down on as a foreigner, who stopped to help the poor man and took him to an inn.

The next day the Samaritan gave the innkeeper two silver coins. "Take care of him, and if you spend more I will pay you when I come back."

"Which of the three behaved like a neighbor?" asked Jesus.

"The one who was kind," the lawyer answered.

Jesus replied, "You go then and do the same."

These stories that Jesus told always had a lesson for his listeners. Jesus said that those who heard his teaching and obeyed it were

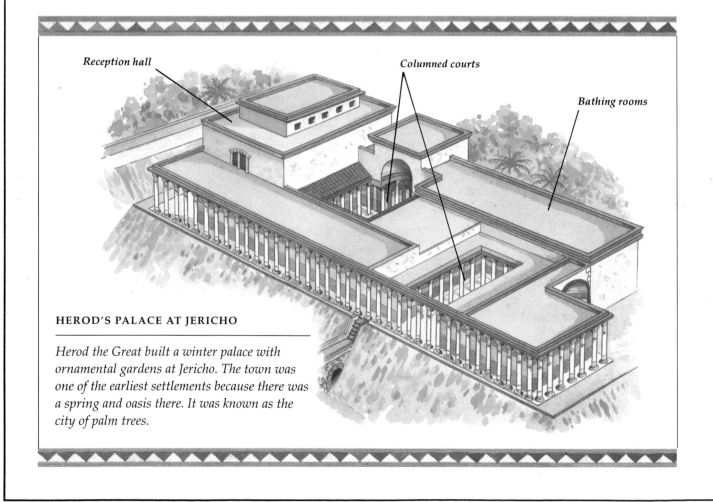

Reception hall

Columned courts

Bathing rooms

HEROD'S PALACE AT JERICHO

Herod the Great built a winter palace with ornamental gardens at Jericho. The town was one of the earliest settlements because there was a spring and oasis there. It was known as the city of palm trees.

Crowds of people were also heading for the city for the Passover Festival, and they spread cloaks and branches of palm trees on the ground for the donkey to walk on. "The king is coming!" they shouted as they welcomed Jesus to Jerusalem.

JESUS ENTERS JERUSALEM

Jesus rode a donkey into Jerusalem and was greeted by a cheering crowd (left).

JESUS TRAVELS SOUTH

Jesus headed south to Jericho, Jerusalem, the capital of Judea, and Bethany, a village nearby where he stayed with friends (below).

like a wise builder who built his house on a rock. When storms and floods came, the house stood firm. Those who ignored his teaching were like a foolish builder who built on sand. His house fell down in the storm.

Near Jerusalem Jesus and his disciples stopped at the village of Bethany. Jesus' friends, Mary, Martha, and their brother, Lazarus, lived there. Martha quickly welcomed Jesus and his disciples and then rushed off to prepare a meal for them. Her sister, Mary, sat down and listened attentively to Jesus' teaching. Martha was annoyed at having to do all the work and asked Jesus to tell Mary to help her. But Jesus told Martha that she was too anxious over things that were less important. Mary had chosen wisely.

As Jesus and his disciples came near Jerusalem, a donkey was brought so that Jesus could ride into the city.

0 10 20 30 40 50 Km
0 10 20 30 Miles

Jordan River

Herod's palace

Jesus on a donkey

Jericho

Jerusalem • Bethany

Martha welcomes Jesus

JUDEA

DEAD SEA

TREACHERY IN JERUSALEM

MATTHEW 26, 27

JERUSALEM was crowded for the Passover Feast. Jesus and his twelve disciples met secretly to share the Passover meal.

"This is the last meal I will share with you," Jesus said. He broke the bread in pieces and passed it around the group with a cup of wine. "This is my body, which is given for you," he said. The disciples were puzzled and sad. Jesus and his friends later walked through the dark streets to a quiet garden called Gethsemane outside the city.

A noisy crowd, armed with swords, clubs, and torches, surged through the olive trees, led by Judas, one of Jesus' disciples.

"The man I kiss is the one you want," said Judas, the traitor, kissing Jesus. Jesus was hustled roughly out of the garden, and his

Wine

Salad of bitter herbs

Lamb

Bread made without yeast

THE PASSOVER FEAST

Each year, at Passover, the Jews celebrated their nation's hasty escape from slavery in Egypt hundreds of years earlier. The traditional meal was roast lamb with a salad of bitter herbs and flat cakes of bread without yeast.

frightened disciples ran away.

Jesus was taken to the High Priest's house where the Jewish council questioned him all night. Finally the High Priest asked Jesus, "Are you the son of God?"

"I am," Jesus replied.

"He is blaspheming. He deserves to die," the council decided.

Then Jesus was taken to the Roman governor, Pilate. Pilate could find no reason to condemn him and sent him to King Herod. Herod sent him back to Pilate. "Shall I let Jesus go?" Pilate addressed a large crowd outside. "No! Crucify him!" they shouted back.

JESUS BETRAYED BY JUDAS

Lights flickered among the shadowy olive trees as a crowd, led by Judas, a disciple of Jesus, surrounded Jesus and took him to be tried and condemned to death (left).

So Jesus was led away to die on a cross outside the city walls. Soldiers hammered nails through his hands and feet and raised the cross with Jesus on it to crucify him.

Jesus said, "Father, forgive them. They don't understand what they are doing." Just before he died he said, "It is finished!" The sky turned black and the earth shook. Jesus' friends asked Pilate for his body. They wrapped it in linen and laid it in a tomb. They rolled a heavy stone across the entrance and went home sadly.

JERUSALEM IN THE TIME OF JESUS

The city of Jerusalem has been in existence since at least 3000 B.C. Herod the Great shaped the city as Jesus knew it, building temples and royal palaces. The Garden of Gesthemane, where Jesus was arrested, was just outside the city. Parts of the garden are still standing today (below).

The main buildings in Jerusalem were:

Herod's palace

The High Priest's house

Temple

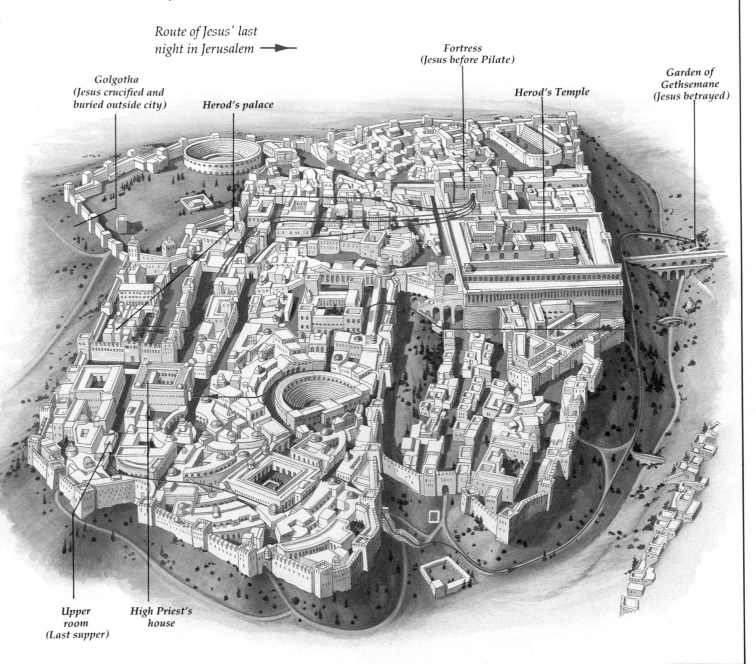

Route of Jesus' last night in Jerusalem ➡

Golgotha
(Jesus crucified and buried outside city)

Herod's palace

Fortress
(Jesus before Pilate)

Herod's Temple

Garden of Gethsemane
(Jesus betrayed)

Upper room
(Last supper)

High Priest's house

JESUS CONQUERS DEATH

MATTHEW 28, LUKE 24, JOHN 20

THE DAY after Jesus had been buried, the Jewish leaders came to ask Pilate, the Roman governor, to put a guard on his tomb. They remembered that Jesus had said he would rise from the dead, and although they did not believe him, they thought his disciples might steal his body and claim that he had risen. Pilate agreed and the guards kept watch.

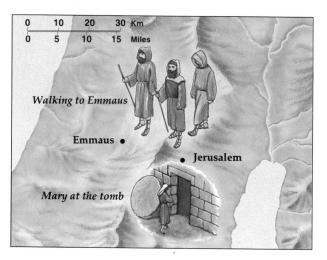

That day was the Sabbath, and none of Jesus' friends went near the tomb. But next morning as day broke, a small group of women went to the tomb with burial spices for the body.

They found that the heavy stone had been rolled away from the entrance, and the body had gone. As they stood there, puzzled, angels appeared. "He is not here. He is risen!" they told the startled women. One of the women, Mary Magdalene, wandered into the garden outside the tomb, crying in confusion. "Why are you crying? Who are you looking for?" a man asked her.

Mary thought he was the gardener and asked him where the body of Jesus had been put. "Mary!" he said, and as she turned to look at him, she knew that it was Jesus. She knelt in front of him and held on to his feet.

"Go and tell the others," Jesus told her gently. So the women hurried away, half frightened and half joyful, to tell the disciples.

The disciples did not believe them, but Peter and John ran off to the tomb to see for themselves. They found that the tomb was indeed empty, the guards had disappeared, and only the burial clothes were left in the tomb. They went back to tell the other disciples the amazing news.

JESUS APPEARS

Soon after his crucifixion, Jesus began to appear before some of his followers, mostly around the Jerusalem area (left).

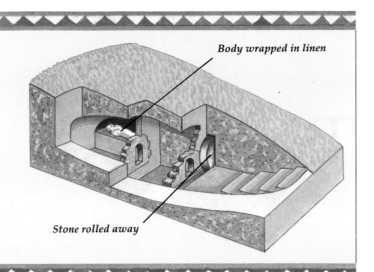
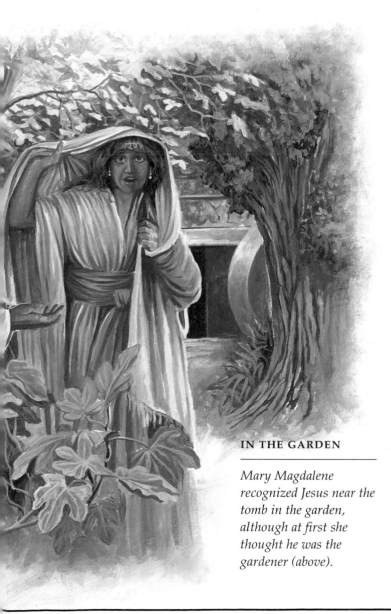

IN THE GARDEN

Mary Magdalene recognized Jesus near the tomb in the garden, although at first she thought he was the gardener (above).

Meanwhile, the frightened guards went back to the city and told the chief priests how there had been an earthquake and an angel had suddenly appeared and rolled back the stone. They had been so terrified, they could do nothing. The priests gave the guards a large sum of money to spread the story that they had fallen asleep and that Jesus' disciples had stolen his body during the night.

Later that day two of Jesus' followers were walking from Jerusalem to their home in Emmaus about seven miles away. As they talked about Jesus and wondered who he really was, a stranger caught up with them and joined in the conversation. He told them that the prophets had foretold that the Messiah would die and rise again.

When they reached Emmaus, they invited the stranger to supper. As he took the bread and said a blessing, they suddenly recognized that it was Jesus, but immediately he disappeared. Excitedly, they rushed back to Jerusalem to tell the other disciples the good news. "Jesus is alive! We've seen him!" they said.

GOOD NEWS FOR THE WORLD

LUKE 24, JOHN 21, ACTS 2

JESUS' DISCIPLES were eating their evening meal when suddenly they were interrupted by the two friends from Emmaus who rushed in to tell them that they had seen the risen Jesus. As they were telling their story, Jesus suddenly appeared in the room and said, "Peace be with you."

At first they were all terrified, thinking he was a ghost, but Jesus reassured them. "Feel me and you will know I am not a ghost," he said. When they saw the scars on his hands and feet from the nails that had fastened him to the cross, they began to believe the wonderful news. "Have you any food?" Jesus asked them, so the joyful disciples shared their supper of cooked fish with him.

Jesus no longer lived with the disciples, but he appeared to them several times in Jerusalem and in Galilee.

One night Peter, James, and John and some other disciples went fishing on the Sea of Galilee as they used to do before they met Jesus. They fished all night but caught nothing, and at sunrise they headed for shore, tired and hungry.

They saw a man standing at the water's edge who called to them to throw their nets out on the right side of the boat. They did, and miraculously the net was so full of fish they could not lift it back into the boat and had to tow it ashore.

"It's Jesus!" John said to Peter. Peter was so excited that he jumped straight into the water and waded ashore. Jesus had lit a fire on the beach.

"Bring some fish," he said, and they ate breakfast together happily.

FISHING IN GALILEE

Fishing was a thriving industry in Galilee. There were fourteen different kinds of fish in the sea. The Galilee fishermen used both small cast nets, which were thrown by hand into shallow water, and large drag nets stretched between two boats. Sudden storms often blew up on this sea, bringing danger to the fishermen.

Forty days after his resurrection, Jesus led his disciples up the Mount of Olives. There he gave them instructions to preach the good news of forgiveness of sins throughout the world, beginning at Jerusalem. But first they were to wait for the power of the Holy Spirit to come upon them. Then Jesus raised his hands in blessing and was taken up to heaven.

The disciples stayed in Jerusalem and met often to pray in the next ten days, along with other followers of Jesus.

Then on the Feast of Pentecost when all the followers gathered together to celebrate the harvest, it was as if a great gust of wind blew through the house. Something like tongues of fire spread out and touched each person.

Suddenly they were able to speak in other languages, and they rushed out and began to talk about Jesus to all the Jews who had come from many countries to Jerusalem for the festival. Some people jeered at them, but many crowded around to listen, and that same day three thousand people were baptized in the name of Jesus and became his followers.

The disciples' task of telling the Good News had begun. Soon there would be followers of Jesus all over the Roman Empire.

ON THE BEACH

Peter waded through the waters of Galilee on recognizing Jesus by the shore (left).

JESUS GATHERS HIS DISCIPLES

Jesus appeared to his eleven disciples (Judas had killed himself) (right).

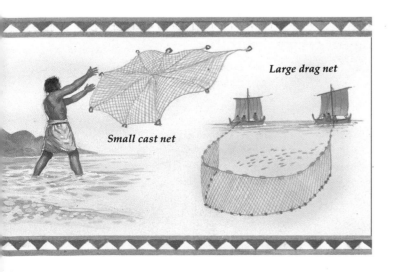

Small cast net

Large drag net

TURNABOUT ON THE DAMASCUS ROAD

ACTS 3, 4, 9

THE NEW followers of Jesus met in one another's homes to share meals and to hear about Jesus. They also went often to the Temple to praise God. One day as Peter and John were going into the Temple, a lame man sitting by the gate begged for money. Peter looked at him. "I have no money, but I give you what I have; in the name of Jesus get up and walk!" he ordered.

Peter reached down and helped the man to stand. At once strength came into his feet and legs, and he started walking. He rushed into the Temple, leaping and jumping and praising God. A crowd quickly gathered and stared in amazement at Peter and John. Peter explained that it was the power of Jesus that had made the lame man walk. When the priests and Jewish leaders heard this, they were furious. They thought they had got rid of Jesus for good. Peter and John were arrested and put in prison.

The Jewish council warned Peter and his friends strongly to stop preaching about Jesus. Peter replied that they had to do what God wanted even if it meant disobeying the Jewish leaders.

As more and more people in Jerusalem became followers of Jesus, the Jewish authorities became more determined to stop them. A man named Saul went to the homes of believers in Jesus and dragged many off to prison. One man, Stephen, was taken out of the city and stoned to death. As a result, some of Jesus' followers fled from Jerusalem to smaller towns in Judea and took the gospel north to Samaria. When Saul realized this was happening, he set off for Damascus with letters of authority from the High Priest to arrest followers of Jesus. He had almost reached the city when suddenly a dazzling light blinded him, and he fell on the ground. "Saul, Saul, why are you attacking me?" a voice asked.

"Who are you, Lord?" the confused Saul replied.

"I am Jesus, whom you are persecuting," the voice said. "Get up and go to Damascus. You will be told what to do there."

In a daze Saul got up, but he still could not see. The men with him led him to the city. He ate no food, and it was three days before his sight was restored.

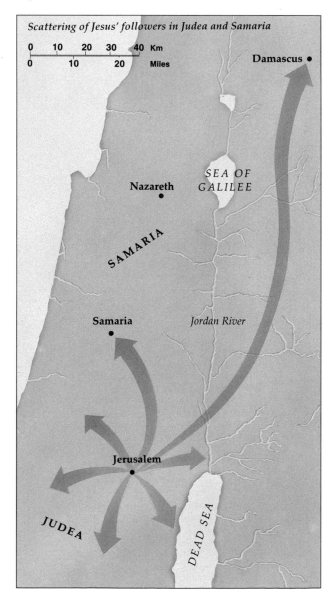

Scattering of Jesus' followers in Judea and Samaria

Saul's life was completely changed. He became a believer in Jesus and joined the others spreading the Good News. He changed his name to the Roman name, Paul, and spent the rest of his life traveling through the countries around the Mediterranean, spreading the message of Jesus.

SAUL SEES THE LIGHT

Saul was converted as a believer when a blinding vision of Christ crossed his path to Damascus, as he went to persecute believers in Jesus (above).

SPREADING THE WORD

After Stephen was stoned to death for being a believer, Jesus' followers began preaching away from Jerusalem into all parts of Judea (left).

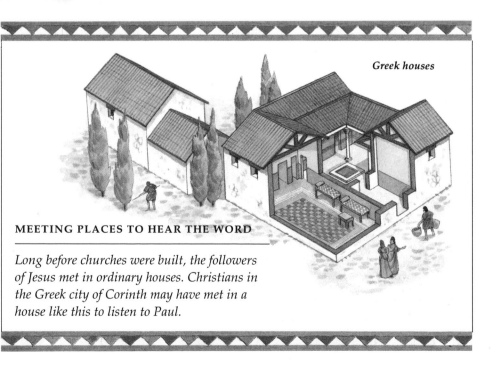

Greek houses

MEETING PLACES TO HEAR THE WORD

Long before churches were built, the followers of Jesus met in ordinary houses. Christians in the Greek city of Corinth may have met in a house like this to listen to Paul.

PAUL'S MISSIONARY ADVENTURES

ACTS 13-28

Paul's journeys

1st journey
2nd journey
3rd journey

ASIA

CRETE

CYPRUS

SYRIA
Antioch

MEDITERRANEAN
SEA

EGYPT

PALESTINE

| 0 | 100 | 200 | 300 | 400 | Km |
| 0 | 50 | 100 | 150 | 200 | Miles |

THE ROMANS built good straight roads throughout their empire. This made it easier for Paul and others to take the gospel to the towns and cities of Asia Minor.

Paul and his friend, Barnabas, spent a year in the city of Antioch in Syria teaching a large group of followers of Jesus. It was here that the believers were first called Christians, probably as a nickname.

Paul and Barnabas then sailed to Cyprus and preached in the Jewish synagogues there. They also sailed to Asia Minor and made their way over high mountain passes into Turkey, persuading many to become Christians.

However, Paul and his companions were not always welcomed, and sometimes their lives were threatened as in Lystra and in Philippi where Paul was beaten and put in jail. But Paul helped groups of believers to form Christian congregations in large cities like Corinth and in many smaller towns.

PAUL'S MISSIONARY JOURNEYS

Between A.D. 46 and A.D. 57, Paul made three great journeys from Antioch, converting people to Christianity (above).

PAUL'S JOURNEY TO ROME

On the way to Rome, Paul was caught in a storm that lasted two weeks. The ship was wrecked, but everyone managed to swim to shore on the island of Malta (right).

PAUL PREACHES

In Athens, Paul preached among the statues of the Greek gods and goddesses in the marketplace (right).

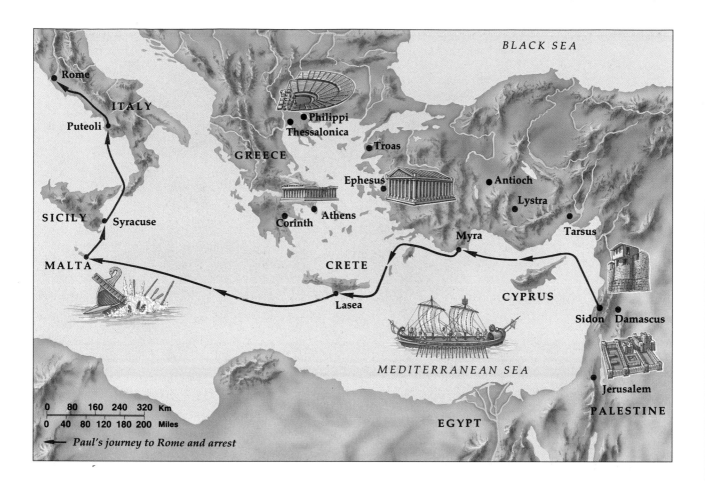

Paul revisited many groups and wrote letters to encourage the new Christians. Several of these letters can be found in the Bible. For example, the book of Ephesians is Paul's letter to the people of Ephesus.

After his third long journey, Paul returned to Jerusalem where he was arrested on a false charge and handed over to the Roman governor at Caesarea. After two years in prison, Paul appealed to be sent to Rome to be tried by the emperor. On the long winter voyage to Rome, the grain ship carrying Paul and other prisoners ran into a furious storm. Paul calmed the frightened crew, and though the ship was wrecked off Malta, everyone survived as Paul had said would happen.

In Rome, Paul was put under house arrest, but still encouraged people to follow the way of Jesus until his death at the order of Emperor Nero, who did his best to stamp out Christianity. He did not succeed.

PAUL'S LETTERS

Jesus' disciples wrote several letters to encourage other people to become Christians. They explained the principles of the Christian way of life to people living in different cities.

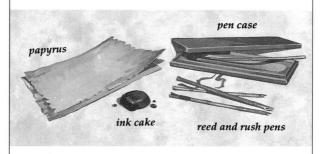

papyrus

pen case

ink cake

reed and rush pens

Paul wrote 13 letters. These are collected in the New Testament. They are: Romans, 1 & 2 Corinthians, Galatians, Ephesians, Philippians, Colossians, 1 & 2 Thessalonians, 1 & 2 Timothy, Titus, and Philemon.

INDEX

Numbers in **bold** refer to maps.
Numbers in *italics* refer to illustrations.